To Mark

From Kenny/Michele.
With Love and Best Wishes
ᵡᵡᵖᵡᵡ

COMMUNICATING WITH
THE WORLD UNSEEN

COMMUNICATING WITH THE WORLD UNSEEN

The Autobiography of a
Spiritualist Medium

JIM CORK

authorHOUSE®

AuthorHouse™
1663 Liberty Drive
Bloomington, IN 47403
www.authorhouse.com
Phone: 1-800-839-8640

Published by AuthorHouse   11/21/2012

ISBN: 978-1-4772-8413-1 (sc)
ISBN: 978-1-4772-8414-8 (e)

Library of Congress Control Number: 2012921949

CONTENTS

To My sister, Sandra, who I love dearly,
to Tony Stapleton, my spiritual mentor,
and to the many people who have
help me through my life.

PREFACE

Over the years many people have asked me how I started as a medium. It would be impossible to explain the whole story in a few minutes, and, I think, boring to hear on its own. Someone suggested I write it down, so I did, and the rest is history, as they say.

Until just recently, I didn't know some of the information regarding Madeline, my biological mother. With a little research, I learnt a great deal about my past, and some of that new information has been included.

To understand a little of how my life has developed over the years, it's important to know where I came from. Because I was adopted at a very young age, I had two families to consider while writing.

For the purpose of this book and to avoid confusion, I will call each set of parents by their first names. My biological parents are Madeline and Jim, and those who adopted me are Lillian and George.

This is not a comprehensive autobiography. When family and friends read it, they may give you information that you didn't know which could have been included. After I finished writing, I also remembered some things that could have been included. I found that by writing my memories down, there was so much I thought I had forgotten, but I found that wasn't true. It's been a journey of pain and joy and a big project with many hours spent sitting, writing, and re-writing, adding information that has just come to light.

I'm not an academic by any standards. Does it matter? No. It's brought me closer to those whom I love dearly and given me a different viewpoint of some of the people that have been with me on this journey.

I have only used first names throughout to protect those whom I have included and wish to remain in the background. Where two people have the same first name, I have used their second initial.

After spending around two years writing from start to finish, I am often asked, 'Would you do it again?' Yes, of course, although I may do it a little differently the second time. It's surprising when you have finished to look back at how much you have written.

I learned so much when I was in the East Lindsey Metaphysical Society (ELMS), the group that I joined and through which I learned a great deal about Spirit and had many spiritual experiences. You will read a little about them in forthcoming chapters.

I am considering writing a book exclusively about ELMS and including what we were taught from Spirit and some of the actual accounts of the group's encounters with Spirit.

I hope you find what you read interesting and that it gives you the encouragement and confidence to live your dream. I have been fortunate in that I have been able to follow and live some of my dreams.

CHAPTER 1

THE BEGINNING

I came into this world on 5 March 1953 in Grimsby, England. I was told this month was very cold, and I wonder if this is why I like the winter more than the summer. It was also the year of many local floods.

My start in life was far from easy. The first thirteen months were traumatic. I was born of Jim and Madeline and was a constant worry. At one point, it looked as if I wouldn't make it due to my poor health.

My parents decided to christen me, and they gave me the name James Arthur Donnelly. I was told this should have been James Patrick Donnelly. This was due to a mix up. I'm not sure who.

Jim was around five feet five inches tall and slim. He had dark hair and was a hard worker. He was born 26 August 1930 in West Hartlepool.

Madeline, his wife, was about five feet two inches tall and also slim. She was soft-spoken and had a nervous disposition. I don't know if she was always nervous or if she developed that trait later on in life.

Jim and Madeline were married for about four years and decided to get divorced. My sister, Sandra, stayed with Madeline, and I was adopted by two loving parents, George and Lillian, around 1954 who were very good to me. I could not have been placed with better parents.

There are rumours and counter-rumours about how Sandra and I were kept in the time we were together. It is alleged that Madeline and her mother drank quite a lot when in each other's company, which I'm told happened regularly, and often neglected us both, even leaving us home alone.

When we wet our nappies, it is alleged they were dried by an open fire and put back on us without being washed. People questioned whether Madeline was fit to be a mother.

Jim came home from work one day to find me crying. Madeline was not in the house, so Jim went to find her. He alleges that she was in someone else's house and afraid to come home, as she did this on numerous similar occasions.

George wanted to have a child with Lillian. Lillian's first husband, Harry, died relatively young of cancer, leaving his and Lillian's children, Barbara, Bill, and Brenda behind.

Lillian was told that she could not have any more children, and if she did, she may have had to choose between her life and the child's. She and George agreed after some time that adoption was the only alternative.

They heard of a child on the same street who was living in dreadful conditions (me). It is alleged that on some occasions, I was left in the alleyway because of my constant crying.

When Madeline and Jim decided to divorce, it was suggested that I be placed with the Salvation Army. Jim was adamantly against this, but as he was working, he couldn't look after me. Social services were eventually involved.

Lillian wrote to Bill, who was in Egypt with the armed forces at the time, to ask if he agreed with the plan to adopt me. She and George thought it only respectful to ask him. He did agree, and the process of adoption began. After all the formalities were finalised, I was adopted by Lillian and George, and my name was changed to James Arthur Cork.

The fight for my life had begun again. I developed double pneumonia and blood poisoning. The doctor told Lillian I would be lucky to survive the next three weeks. For those three weeks, Lillian sat up and nursed me through it. She was exhausted, but her prayers were answered, and I started to pick up. I wasn't ready to go home to Spirit just yet. As I look back at some of the early pictures of myself, it seems incredible that I went through so much in such a short period of time.

Lillian and George didn't have much money, as they now had four children to consider. My adoptive siblings were several years older than me; however, as the baby of the family, I was spoiled in the right way.

Lillian was a hard worker in her day. If I remember correctly, she worked in the fish house and on the land.

They didn't have the machines we have today to plant or pick potatoes when working on the land. She sat on the back of a plough-like machine, and as it carved out furrows, she dropped potatoes in a certain distance apart. Then two blades at the back of the machine covered them over.

Lillian was around five feet seven inches tall, and George was slightly taller. Both were of slim build. George had worked as a minesweeper during the War. After the war was over, he did various jobs and could turn his hand to almost anything.

When I was old enough, Brenda, Lillian's daughter, often took me to the open market in Freeman Street, Grimsby. These were mostly on Saturdays, as didn't work that day. I always came away with some toy; it may have only been small, but as they say, it's the thought that counts.

Brenda was always a good worker. She wasn't afraid to roll her sleeves up and get stuck in, as it were. One job was in a lemonade bottling plant. I remember her taking me there once. I was fascinated by the production line with the bottles passing me and being filled. It was noisy, and the floor was wet. Nowadays under Health and Safety, the workers in such a plant would wear ear defenders. Looking back, I am sure there were two factories, different companies, bottling lemonade and other soft drinks in Grimsby.

Housing at that time was primitive by today's standards. This could have been the cause of many children's illnesses. No central heating or running hot water. To have a bath, we heated water in a copper boiler with a gas ring underneath. The bath itself was made of tin, and they came in different sizes: some weren't quite big enough for you to lie in, only to sit in. I only remember the one that I used.

The toilet was outside. Imagine in the depth of winter getting out of a warm bed, going downstairs and outside, chipping ice off the latch, and finally sitting on a freezing seat. That's how it was for many years. I can tell you, you didn't hang around in the loo.

Most of the rooms in our house had open-grate fires which burned coal. To light them, first you put paper in the grate at the bottom, then wood on top, and coal on top of that. Then you lit the paper, which in turn burned the wood and then the coal. All of this took time; however, once the coal was hot, the fires did throw a lot of heat out and were a good light source.

If you went to the corner shop and bought fresh bread, put a piece on your toasting fork, and held it in front of the fire grate, it made fantastic toast. Bread buns were toasted in the same way. Fresh bread yielded the best results.

It was common in those days for a married son or daughter to share the same house as their parents until they were allocated a council house. You had to be wealthy to afford a private house.

When Brenda married John, they lived in the front room, often called the 'best room'. Lillian and George lived in the middle room, which was next to the kitchen. Everyone shared the kitchen, and we sat together for most meals.

The next six years were hard because my body was slow to develop, and I had several stays in hospital. Although I was very young, I do remember being in Louth Hospital for a short while. I was taken to a room and asked to put on dark glasses and to take my shirt off. I was told not to look at the light slightly to my right but to look straight ahead.

There was this strange smell a few seconds after the lights were turned on. I now know these lights gave off ultraviolet radiation and were called 'sunshine lights' then. Thousands of people now go to tanning studios and lie in sunbeds, which use fluorescent tubes and are much safer than the bulbs of the sunshine lights.

I was also slow to learn, and some thought that I may have been retarded, as my concentration drifted regularly.

Lillian took me to the doctor's at some stage and asked for his opinion. He said I wasn't retarded. I just needed a lot of love, care, and attention.

My first school was in Strand Street, Grimsby. The playground was on top of the building. As far as I know, this arrangement is unusual today because of Health and Safety. A small building in a corner took up part of the playground. I'm not sure what it was used for. I think it's possible it housed the lift equipment.

If I remember correctly, the kitchen was on the second floor and the canteen was on the ground floor. There was a dumb waiter, which was a small wooden cabinet with a rope on either side. You pulled the right-hand rope for up and the left-hand one for down.

My first teacher was Miss House. One day, our class were brought into a room where we were told that she had died. Being around six years of age, I couldn't understand this. I just thought that she would never come back.

When I was around nine years of age, my family had to move, as the council were pulling our house down. Most of the houses on the street were being demolished to make way for several sixteen-storey high-rise flats.

Lillian and George were offered a detached prefab on what is called the Nunsthorpe Estate. This area was originally nicknamed 'Garden City' because the houses had been built as temporary accommodation after the war with plenty of garden space in back and in front. My sister Brenda and her husband were offered number 5, and Lillian and George 15, and naturally, they didn't refuse.

The new house was a dream in every sense of the word. The coal-fire-heated water in the copper boiler tank supplied hot running water to the kitchen and bathroom, which was inside. No more chipping ice off the latch of the toilet as at the old house.

There were also a built-in fridge and cooker. Compared to where we had been living, this was heaven. There was plenty of garden space for Lillian to grow flowers, which she loved, plus hedges on three sides of the prefab. George loved it because there was enough room for him to have a little veggie patch.

CHAPTER 2

ADOPTION

I was told from a very early age that I was adopted. When Madeline, Lillian, and George went to court, the judge told Lillian and George to make sure I was told I was adopted. It has to be appreciated that the rules and regulations of adoption around 1954 were different from what they are today.

When I was about twelve years old, we had a painting lesson at school. Not that I was very good, but I took my painting home and showed it to Lillian. I told her that I wanted to show my mother. 'I am your mother,' she replied. 'No! My real mother,' I shouted. This must have hurt, but if it did, she didn't show it. It must have been like I was throwing all she had done for me back in her face. It was at this point that Lillian and George decided that the time was right to satisfy my curiosity further, as I had often asked questions about my biological parents.

They had told me some things about my biological parents and how I was adopted, but they left out some of the finer details. They may have thought I was too young at that stage to fully understand. I'm sure they were right, as it can be difficult at that age to comprehend the complications and facets of relationships.

It was quite some time after this that Lillian and George found my biological father. I was, of course, apprehensive.

After spending a couple of hours with him, it was clear that he didn't know what to say to me and vice versa. Lillian and George did most of the talking. Jim asked me about school and how I was doing and what my interests were.

There were many questions that I wanted to ask but didn't. It would be many years after that meeting that some of them would be answered. Looking back, I don't know what I expected. Did I think he was just going to pour his heart out? I would have been misguided to think so.

I left not knowing what to think. The one thing I needed now was time. I didn't feel any emotion. On the way home, I just sat and looked out of the bus window. Lillian and George asked me if I was all right an hour or so after we arrived home. I said I was, but it would take me a long time to sort my feelings out in my head.

Approximately forty-five years later, at the time of writing this book, Jim finally told me what led to his and Madeline's divorce.

All down the years I asked myself the same questions over and over and trying to find the answers. You always feel that some questions need answers. But I know I will never know the full truth because some of the people that could help are in the spirit world. Thinking about it, I wonder, would knowing the answers solve anything? I don't think so. This is one of those roads that everyone has to walk alone if adopted.

A meeting was also arranged by Lillian and George to meet with my biological mother, Madeline. When I met her, I thought she was more approachable than Jim. I didn't feel as awkward with her, and she asked me quite a lot of questions. Like with Jim, I wanted to ask her many questions but didn't. I wonder if I was afraid to know the answers.

No one likes to think they are not liked or wanted. My top question was, had I been wanted, and if not, why? As many before me who have been in the same situation have asked, I wanted to know, was I an accident? Even if that was the case, didn't I need the same love as a wanted child? What about Sandra, my biological sister? Had she been wanted, or was she an accident as well? She too needed to be loved and to feel wanted as any child should be. It's far better not to have been born than to be neglected or not wanted.

Over the next few months, I occasionally visited both Jim and Madeline. I didn't bring up the past in case the two told me conflicting stories. Although my visits were infrequent, our communication did get easier, and Madeline and I formed a bond. It was stronger than the one I had with Jim, but this was to change later.

I didn't tell Lillian or George I visited Jim or Madeline. I didn't want Lillian or George to think that

I might go back to my birth parents. This would have broken their hearts, I'm sure.

Lillian asked me on several occasions if I'd seen anything of them. I always thought of an excuse. I'm not one for lying, as I was always told that liars have to have good memories.

I'm sure Lillian suspected that I had seen them, as I was always home to watch wrestling on TV on a Saturday afternoon, and sometimes when I visited Madeline or Jim, I would arrive home only just before the wrestling started.

Lillian, George, and I watched wrestling together, as we loved it, even though some of it may have been put on for show. Like Sunday dinner, it was a ritual. I loved those days and sometimes wish I could go back to them.

I cannot remember when I first met Sandra, but I think it was at Madeline's. I remember our meeting being awkward, as once again, what do you talk about with someone who you haven't seen or heard from in many years? You can never make up for those lost years or regain experiences like brother and sister fighting over the least little thing that we would have shared. We would not have such memories to share or talk about later. Physical scars heal, even thought they may leave a mark, mental ones never do.

Sandra and I now talk about the past quite regularly and what might have been if we had stayed together. I had the better life, and it hurts me to see that Sandra's painful memories haunt her even today.

In conversation with Sandra about this book, she told me she often thought about what I was doing and where I was when she was young.

To go back a little, I found out about having a sister by accident. When I was at school, my mate and I delivered Christian Aid envelopes to people's doors. On one particular day, a woman shouted, 'Jimmy!'

I turned round and couldn't see anyone.

My mate said, 'I think she's shouting to you.'

I replied, 'Who is it? I can't see anyone.'

Pointing to a window in a flat, my mate said, 'It's her, in the flats.'

Then the woman shouted, 'Jimmy, over here! I want to speak to you.'

Walking over to the window she was leaning from, I told my mate I had never seen her before.

'Well, she knows you, all right,' he replied.

'You don't recognise me, do you?' the woman said.

I looked at her more intently. 'No, I'm sorry, I don't.' I couldn't see her fully, as the window obscured her lower half.

'I'm your auntie Betty. Has the mum who brought you up told you everything?' she said with a slight smile.

'Yes,' I replied.

'I have a picture of you and your sister on the sideboard.' This caught me by surprise, to say the least.

'I haven't got a sister,' I told her.

Betty then turned and walked to her sideboard. She returned with something in her hand.

My mate and I turned to each other and shrugged. Betty showed me a photograph of Sandra and myself.

'Obviously she hasn't told you everything. Take that with you and show her. Your mom may have her reasons for not telling you. Bring it back the next time you're passing.'

I took the photograph, put it in my pocket, and carried on. Once we finished delivering envelopes, we headed home. My mate and I discussed what had happened for what seemed ages. We couldn't understand why such an important thing like this had been withheld from me.

When I arrived home, I told Lillian what had happened, and she denied that I had a sister at first. A long heated discussion followed, and eventually she admitted that she had kept this information from me. The atmosphere wasn't very good for a couple of days. I think mainly because Lillian was not honest when I first asked her. I am not one to hold a grudge, so things did go back to normal. Well, as normal as they could be.

I can't appreciate how Lillian and George must have felt then. After all, my curiosity was getting deeper. I think they knew this time would come. I suppose every adoptive parent must worry about when their adopted or fostered child needs to be told about their birth families and, in my case, the finer details about them.

The problem I had was whether to believe what else they had told to me if they could keep something as important as this from me, whatever their reasons. I believe that this was the only thing they kept back. Even so, once a seed of doubt has been planted, it casts doubts on other things that you learn in the future.

Madeline and her third husband, Reg, were blessed with a daughter, Jackie. Sandra would be taking a back seat, as it were, for many years to come as they grew up.

Reg promised Madeline the earth only to be disappointed once more. Sandra spent the last part of her childhood very unhappy.

Sandra has told me that Madeline would often have a black eye, bruised ribs, or other injuries inflicted by the hands of her second and third husbands. She often lied and said that she had walked into a door or fallen down.

Reg sent Jackie to two private schools to give her a good education. I'm not sure of the duration. This, of course, would have made Sandra feel even more inferior.

While Jackie had the best clothes, most of the time, Sandra walked around almost in rags. It is my understanding that Reg's job wasn't the best paying, and private schools are expensive, so it is alleged that Reg paid for Jackie's tuition fees with money from nefarious sources.

When a man takes a wife who already has children, and vice versa, the children from the previous marriage often suffer. Some children feel their step-parents favour their own children over those of their new spouse.

Also, when Reg came on the scene, he labelled Sandra a trouble maker, and she often saw Reg's hand across her face and other parts of her body. Sandra does admit that she was a little rebellious due to having three fathers, more so when Reg married Madeline.

Sandra, Jackie, and Reg's relationship was rocky to say the least.

In 1967, at the tender age of sixteen, Sandra fell pregnant. Madeline found out and confronted her. Rather than being supportive, Madeline made her feel dirty and guilty. Madeline and Reg told her that she couldn't keep the baby. If she didn't give it up for adoption, Sandra could pack her bags and go.

I think from what I have been told that this was Reg's decision more than Madeline's. Madeline went along with Reg because she was frightened of him, as her diary confirms.

Society was very different in 1967 than it is today. There wasn't as much support for young, unmarried mothers. Parents were concerned about the shame the family would feel from neighbours who knew that their daughter was having a baby without the support of the father and without being married first. Reg told the father of Sandra's baby to stay well away.

As Sandra got bigger, she was sent away to Spalding, a maternity home. Many parents did this. The daughters would return home minus the baby. Life would carry on as best as possible on their return, and relatives would avoid any awkward questions.

Jackie was around five years old when Sandra was sixteen and sent away. Jackie started fretting soon after. When Sandra was brought home, the situation was far from ideal, as there was tension within the family. While Sandra was away at Spalding for that short period, it was alleged that Madeline and Reg went on holiday.

Like any loving mother, which Sandra was, she had developed a bond with the baby. Six weeks after the birth, Sandra took her baby girl for a walk. Crying most of the way and alone, Sandra saw her baby for the last time. She then went through the trauma of handing over her baby girl to the authorities.

The father of Sandra's baby daughter, given the chance, may have been a wonderful dad. But we will never know what he felt. I wonder if he thinks about the daughter he never saw after the adoption.

There is one surviving photograph of Sandra holding her beautiful baby girl. Because I wasn't there at the time or of an age of understanding, it's difficult for me to judge other people's situations. We need to put ourselves in their shoes, and then, and only then, may we have some idea of what they were going through.

Even when Sandra was at Spalding, Madeline and Reg didn't go to see her. I cannot imagine what she must have been going through, all alone except for the midwife and other medical personnel. What made matters worse was that I wasn't there to help her through all this.

Several years later, Sandra married and had two beautiful children, Tracy and Lee, who are both a credit to her. She and her husband, William, gave Tracy and Lee what they hadn't had when they were growing up: unconditional love, care, and attention. After around thirty three years of marriage, Sadly, William, affectionately known as Bill or Billy, died after a short illness. Naturally, this has left a big hole in the family, as they were very close.

The one thing I missed when I was growing up was not having any brothers or sisters near my own age to play with or share my toys. My adoptive siblings were several years older than I. I must say, however, that Bill, Brenda, and Barbara were very good. They bought me what other children could only dream of.

The youngest child in any family, especially whose brother and sisters are quite a few years older, can have a very lonely life. It would hurt sometimes when I saw other children playing at school with their brothers and sisters.

I would not find out until many years later that I was the only one in both my families to be called to

Spirit's service. However, I have heard that Madeline's mother read the cards and tea leaves.

Lillian and George weren't religious and didn't go to church. They had their own thoughts on the subject and kept these to themselves most of the time. They left it to me as I was growing up to decide which religion I wanted to embrace.

CHAPTER 3

THE MOVE

Most mediums will tell you that they had spirit friends as children. I didn't. When I was young, my bedroom was upstairs in the back of a terrace house. The docks were about a five-minute walk away.

I use to be frightened by the noises of the dock workers and cranes as they loaded and unloaded the ships throughout the quiet night. I would often pull the bedcovers over my head. Of course, after a while, I just fell asleep.

When I was around eight years old, our house was due to be pulled down to make way for several blocks of sixteen-storey flats. Both Lillian and Brenda were offered prefab houses on the Nunsthorpe Estate around 1962 which we all excepted.

The prefabs were similar in size to bungalows and their exterior and interior walls were made of cement fibres. It was rumoured that the walls were made of asbestos; however, when the council decided to modernise the interiors of the prefabs many years later, they found the words 'Made in the USA' printed inside the walls.

Some prefabs in Grimsby with tin walls still stand. Most of the prefabs made of cement fibres have been pulled down. I think only two are standing because when Lillian and George were offered the chance of buying them, one or two other residents did, but we didn't. One hundred pounds was a great deal of money at that time. I do not remember what year this was.

It was a big move for our family. Everyone was excited because it meant that Brenda and her husband, John, could have their own place. The prefabs were detached from each other, making them even better. Each had two bedrooms, one nice large living room, a good-sized kitchen, and the best part, an inside bathroom and toilet. Brenda and John lived at number 5, and Lillian, George, and I at number 15.

Although it took quite a while to settle down, our new house was heaven compared to what we had been used to. Hundreds would be still living as we had been for many years to come.

My appetite picked up. No longer did I pick at my food and look pale. I ate almost everything on my plate. Along with my colour, attention span improved. Some say it was because of the fresh air because our new neighbourhood was so open.

In the summer, I could see the sun set lower on the horizon than where we had been living. Some people in our old street didn't want to move, as they had been there for many years. Quite a few had been born in the houses where they lived. Several died not long after moving. I think the change was too much for them at their age.

I moved to a different school as well, which for a nine-year-old is a big upheaval. Once I saw the house's garden, I knew the move was well worth it. I hadn't been into gardening at the old house, as the garden there was more or less just a small strip. In the prefab, the front garden was just as big as the back one.

Lillian loved flowers, and now she was able to grow her own. It wasn't long before she was growing tomatoes, cucumbers, and quite a few other vegetables. In fact, she had to buy another fridge-freezer she was growing so much.

George was in his element. He loved growing potatoes, rhubarb, broad beans, and runner beans. We were all very happy in the new neighbourhood, especially Brenda and John.

CHAPTER 4

ORTHODOX
CHURCH

I joined St Martin's Church choir in Grimsby when I was around ten years old. I didn't find religion; it found me. I just felt I wanted to go to church, and St Martin's was quite near to where I lived. I loved it. However, I was asked to leave after I got into a fight. I was not the fighting kind, usually; it is not part of my philosophy. My friend was being picked on.

He was not the kind to defend himself, and I thought someone had to take a stand, so I did. I punched the bully several times. I wasn't proud of my actions then or now.

I had a strong faith then but didn't vocalise it. After the fight, I didn't tell Lillian or George the real reason why I was no longer attending church. I think I said that I wasn't happy there. It seemed better just to pass it off in that way.

After a short time, I started attending the other nearby church, which was about a seven-minute walk from where I lived in the other direction from St Martin's. I didn't like it as much because it was a more modern church, with chairs instead of pews and a plain altar.

A Franciscan friar visited once. I would be around ten or eleven years old. I had been interested in the monastery life but hadn't considered joining until his visit. After I talked to him, the life seemed very appealing, maybe because it was simple and seemed to offer a closer relationship to God.

His was not a closed order, as they called it. They worked the land and sold their produce on the open market to pay their way in part. In a closed order, the monks do not come out of the monastery unless they need to. I would think the life in a closed order is stricter than an open one, but I'm no expert.

Once Lillian found out that I was considering joining, she put on her coat and rushed round to the vicarage and told the vicar that in no way was I going into any monastery.

I tried to make her understand that I had not made a definite decision. After I explained that I was only enquiring, she said that she would go round again and give the vicar another piece of her mind for putting such notions in my head.

It's a hard life being a monk, I was told, giving up all you own to live in a disciplined order. It's a big decision to make and shouldn't be taken likely.

I sometimes wonder how far I would now be spiritually if I had joined the order. It wasn't the path I was meant to walk, obviously, and only on hindsight can I know this.

It's a pity we can't see very far into the future sometimes. If we could, maybe then would we choose to take another path. But in another breath, I have to say, it's good that we can't see that far ahead, as we may miss some vital lessons that we are here to learn if we could.

I believe the road we are on is the road we were meant to walk down. We all have lessons to learn, some hard and others easy.

In one way, I envy the monk's lifestyle even though it's a hard life. My reasons run very deep.

One film that I love watching is *The Nun's Story*' Although it's about nuns, it shows in part what kind of lifestyle they have agreed to live. I also think that Audrey Hepburn and Peter Finch were well matched in the film.

CHAPTER 5

FIRST SPIRITUAL AWAKENING

I was tired and went to bed just a little earlier than usual. I think I was around fourteen years old. I lay there not thinking of anything in particular and trying to go to sleep. For some reason, a dreadful fear that I was going to die came over me. It was so intense that I started to cry. I said in my mind, 'Please, God, don't let me die. I don't want to die.' I said this over and over as I continued to cry. I also remember thinking that the blackness of the room had a warmth to it which I had not felt before, I don't know why. After some time, I fell asleep.

The next day, I went over this event in my mind, looking for triggers that might have set this kind of emotion off. Nothing came to mind. I wonder if, in the deep recesses of my mind, memories from when I was given about three weeks to live were coming up from my subconscious. Although they may not have conscious thought as we know it at such an early age, even infants yearn for survival.

I didn't have many close friends when I was young. I had more acquaintances than anything else. I spent a lot of time alone in my bedroom playing records or reading.

Suddenly, while listening to a record in my bedroom, I felt someone watching me from over my left shoulder. I turned around, and, of course, there was no one there. I turned to the front again but still felt someone watching me. As I slowly backed up until my back was flat against the bedroom wall, the person over my left shoulder seemed to melt right through the wall and into the other bedroom. It was a strange feeling. Even though my back was against the wall, I felt as if I could see into the other room.

It frightened me, as I didn't know what had happened. I left my bedroom in a hurry, wanting to get out as fast as possible.

When I went into the living room, Lillian asked me what was wrong and said my face was as white as a sheet.

I didn't speak to anyone about this, as I thought they may think that there was something wrong with me. Over the next few months, this happened regularly, and the feeling was always the same. The strange thing is that although I didn't know who it was that was visiting me, as I do now, I always knew that it was the same person.

I realise now that I had nothing to be frightened of. This was merely the first time I had a change of conscious perception, that I sensed other vibrations around me.

One particular day, Lillian was not quite with it when I came home from school. You just know when things seem to be different or not right with your mother. She served tea as usual, washed up, and sat down. I asked her what was wrong. She said that my grandmother, Lillian's mother, was very ill, and had been told that the doctors didn't think she would make it.

I cannot remember what age my grandmother would have been at that time. I think possibly in her seventies. I told Lillian that I was going out on my push bike for a while, and I went down to the house of the minister, where I was almost barred for fighting and knocked on his door.

I asked him if it would be all right if I went into the church and prayed for a while and explained my reason for asking. Strangely, he asked me if I thought it would do any good. I told him that when I had prayed for other people before, most of the time my prayers had been answered in some way.

The church had wooden pews showing years of wear. They were so highly polished you could almost see your face in them. It was filled with the strong smell of incense, which I loved. I looked up at the beautiful silver cross on the altar that was large enough to be seen clearly from the back.

After about fifteen of minutes praying and thinking, I left. I felt a little better and went straight home. Lillian told me that she didn't think it would be long before Gran died. I'm sure we both had a lump in our throats then. I told her she would pull through this time but that Spirit would take her the next time.

I don't know how I knew that then. I just did. Lillian asked me where I got the information from. I couldn't give her an answer, as I didn't know myself.

About two days later, Gran starting picking up. I was pleased, as I was close to her. Lillian asked me again afterwards how I knew she would be all right; again I couldn't give her an answer.

Lillian suffered from headaches and earaches quite a lot of the time. She never went out without a headscarf on, otherwise she would come home with a very bad earache.

One beautiful day, I came home from school to find Lillian in pain with a very bad headache, worse than usual. It must have been very bad because she didn't have anything ready for tea. That wasn't like Lillian; she always had tea ready on the table when I got home.

I told her I was going into the garden for a while as it was still light out. Our front garden was quite large and had several borders full of flowers. While I was sorting out one side of the border, I asked in my mind for her headache to be taken away.

After about ten minutes, I went back inside. I said to Lillian, 'Your headache has started to go.' Her reply didn't surprise me: 'How can you have known that?' I now understand how I knew and who was helping.

It wasn't long before other people with worse conditions than headaches asked me to help them.

Colin, probably my only friend at school then, wanted to learn to play the piano and asked me if I wanted to learn as well. My first problem was that my family didn't have a piano. The second was whether Lillian would be able to afford the lessons.

I spoke to Lillian about it, and amazingly, she said yes. John knew of a piano going cheap, and within a couple of weeks, we had the piano delivered and the music lessons booked.

Colin learned very fast, and I'm sure he would have made a good pianist. While he, his brother Barry, and their father were returning from a fishing trip, they were involved in a car accident. Supposedly Barry lost control of the car while trying to negotiate a bend. Tragically, Colin died. Both Barry and his father survived the crash.

Seat belts weren't compulsory in those days. Colin's mother wanted him to go to bingo that day, and he nearly did but changed his mind to go fishing at the last minute. Colin's dad had had a little too much to drink in the pub on the way home and asked Barry to drive.

My music teacher heard of what I was doing. I still don't know how she found out. I might have said something about it during one of my lessons at one point.

Her husband suffered from asthma, and at times it was quite bad. After one of my piano lessons, she asked me if I would ask for him to feel better. For the first time, I knew just after she asked me that I felt they could not cure him but would offer him some relief.

At the next week's lesson, my teacher told me that her husband had improved quite a lot. I was pleased those I asked could do something for him. My teacher and her family were very nice people. Her husband played the violin and their son the drums. Apparently all three performed gigs and were very well respected.

A few weeks after I asked for relief for my teacher's husband, I was making quite a lot of mistakes in my playing, but my teacher didn't correct me on most of them. I asked her if there was anything wrong. She said that her arthritis was playing up and that she was in quite a lot of pain.

At the end of the lesson, I told her that when I came back next week, the pain would be gone.

I didn't think at all about how things would turn out. Once again, I just knew she would see some improvement.

These events further strengthened my faith and my belief in a God force.

There were many other instances in which I interceded for pain relief and, in some cases, cures and they took place. However, I couldn't help some people no matter how much I asked for them. I never thought then or now that I was responsible for anything. All I did was ask on these people's behalf. It was a beautiful feeling to hear of the relief people received.

When I felt that people would receive only relief, it did sadden me; however, I was grateful for any help given to them. I didn't then and I don't now take it for granted. I didn't talk to anyone about what was happening. For one thing, I didn't know anyone, and second, where would it lead if I did?

I was concerned, however, when I was asked to intercede for someone with cancer. This was something else altogether. Asking for relief for a headache or backache was one thing, cancer was a different ball game.

This person expected so much from me. What if, when I asked, that I felt that they couldn't do anything? How would I feel? Could I handle it, being so young?

Many thoughts went through my head, even as young I was. Some of the questions revolved around what would happen if my request didn't work this time.

I had seen several programmes on the television regarding faith healing. These explained that it was the patient's faith that made him or her well and not the healer. This is different to spiritual healing.

Spiritual healing it doesn't require a patient to have faith. Instead, the healer channels energy from Spirit to the patient. Even if the healer feels a little off, the energy is still transferred to the patient.

Keeping a positive attitude does help. This goes a long way for a patient, whichever form of healing he or she chooses, and there are many different forms.

Some people swear by crystal healing while others love working with colour. I don't think it matters as long as we can reach the same result.

I wasn't sure where I would go from here or how far my healing would take me. I didn't know anyone else who I could talk to on the subject. Although my first love was medicine, I eventually went to sea and out of the situation.

CHAPTER 6

CAREERS

I don't know about other schools, but my senior one had a careers day on which students were asked to attend a meeting to discuss what we would like to do after leaving school with a person that would help us choose our careers and hopefully point us in the right direction.

My first love was medicine. I loved biology and nearly always came out on top in my class, even though my grades were down in other subjects.

My second love was film and the stage. I asked about carers in both these industries. Unfortunately, because I was a slow learner and had missed quite a lot of school for one reason or another, my maths and English were holding me back. I must be quite honest—I hated maths. I didn't hate English as much, but we weren't taught about grammar.

The counsellor told me that my chances of becoming a doctor were remote; however, he suggested that I go into the forces as a medic. I applied to the Royal Air Force and was given a date to go to Lincoln to sit the entrance exam. About six of us applied, but not all for the same position.

I was the first to be called into the office after the exam. I walked into the examiner's small room.

'Please sit down,' he said. I don't remember what he looked like, as it was a long time ago. 'I'm sure you know why I have asked you in first.'

I thought I did and put on a brave face. 'I have an idea,' I replied.

'I'll come to the point. I'm sorry to say that you have failed the entrance exam. You have not been the first and you will not be the last.' The examiner lifted his head slightly. 'If you want to re-apply, I would suggest that you go to college for two years to study maths and English because those subjects are what let you down.'

I was gutted.

'Maths and English are very important in the medical corps, as I'm sure you can appreciate. Thank you for applying, and we hope to see you again in the future.'

I left as soon as I could to catch the train home.

When I walked through the door at home, Lillian knew by my expression that I had failed. I told her what the exam consisted of and then just broke down. She consoled me the best way she could, as she knew medicine was important to me. We had a good discussion afterwards, and I explained that I did not want to go to college for two years.

How many times have we looked back and said, 'If I could go back, I would change things'? When I look back, I think service in the medical corps was not to be but that I was inspired to take the road that I took.

It was just afterwards that I decided to go into the Merchant Navy. After all, I had no qualifications, and service would relieve the pressure of people asking for healing, especially cancer. I would have liked to have gone fishing; however, the risk was too high, as I lost friends at sea.

CHAPTER 7

TIME TO LEAVE HOME AND GO TO SEA

I couldn't go to the Merchant Navy training college in Kent until I was sixteen and a half. Between the time I left school and reaching sixteen, I worked in a box making factory.

It was quite an easy job; I just had to be focused on what I was doing. The job was to last only six months, so I thought, why not? As it happened, I loved it.

I needed to get away and have some space and a good long think. The Merchant Navy certainly would give me that. I was given a date to leave Grimsby for Kent and the 'concrete ship', as they affectionately called the training college for the deck and catering crews.

The catering training program, which I applied for, was an eight-week course, and deck-work training program was a twelve-week course. Apart from staying at a youth camp on a school holiday some years before and spending one or two weeks in hospital, I had not been away from home on my own. I would now be away for eight weeks, and I was concerned. I think anyone in a similar situation would feel the same.

I took the train to Kent, and a small coach met me at the other end. It was only a short journey to the college, which looked very big as we approached.

I enjoyed the course and made one or two friends while I was there. I kept in touch with several of the other students for quite a long time afterwards. The eight weeks soon passed, and it was time to say goodbye to everyone.

I returned home and signed on at the Merchant Navy ship allocation building. After two weeks at home, I was allocated a position on the *Bellness*, a brand-new ship sailing from Scotland.

Because the *Bellness* was a passenger cargo ship, my allocation would give me more experience than serving on only a cargo ship. There was plenty to do once I was on board, including learning to fit in with a team: Bill, the cook; Ron, the second cook and baker; Barry and Criss, the two stewards for the officers; and the other cabin boy, who I would be bunking with.

The other cabin boy looked after the deck crew and served them at mealtimes. It was my job to take the orders from the two stewards and pass them to the cook. Once the order was complete, I would bring the plates to the stewards so they could serve the meals to the officers or passengers.

Every Sunday, the captain came round to inspect each work area. He used a pair of white gloves to wipe over areas of his choice. If he found any debris or dust anywhere, you would have to clean the whole of your work area again. Hygiene on board ships is essential.

While I was in Spain, I bought a classical guitar. One of the deck crew who could play offered to teach me, and I must admit, I did very well. Once we had finished for the day, we had quite a bit of time to kill. I went on the deck to my favourite spot, where it was nice and quiet, and would practise for hours.

Crew members needed a hobby of some kind. Some spent many hours writing letters. We couldn't bring along a typewriter every time you went to join a ship, so they wrote everything by hand.

I was very lucky in that I visited many countries and saw different cultures. I served for just the one trip, which lasted nine months.

During the course of the trip, I had a small breakdown caused by a combination of things. The problem was that I couldn't just get off and call at the doctor's.

The chief cook had a go at me for some trivial matter. I went back to my work area and starting smashing up plates and things. I then burst into tears and sobbed uncontrollably. Several people rushed in to see what all the fuss and noise was about. They called the medic, and it was obvious to him that I was going through an emotional breakdown.

It took me about three weeks to come round, and even then not completely, as I was more quiet than I had been before. I went back to work, but nothing was the same.

I often walked down to the bow of the ship and looked over the side. Not only was this relaxing, but I could be on my own. It was a good place to think.

It was amazing to look over the side. On occasion, as far as I could see, the water would be flat. Then, quickly, the ship would be in the middle of a storm. It was amazing to watch nature in all its glory. In some areas of the world, flying fish would swim alongside the ship. This was also amazing.

It was important to keep in touch with everyone back home. As there was plenty of time to write letters, I made sure they were posted the next time we were in port. Although I didn't know Sandra that well then, I still made sure I wrote to her.

When I'm asked which country I liked most, I had to say the United States of America. The people were so friendly, and nothing was too much trouble for them. The other question I'm asked is, why did you leave after just one trip?

There are many reasons, but sixteen and a half was too young to leave the homestead for me.

In conversation with Sandra about this book, I mentioned including my stint in the Merchant Navy. She brought out all the letters I wrote to her. There was even a 100-yen note in an envelope I sent to her from Japan. It's in excellent condition. I read some of the letters, and they brought many memories flooding back.

I met some amazing people while away. The first time we went to the United States, there were street sellers on the quayside. One chap was selling tapestries of the Last Supper. They were so beautiful that I bought one. I saw it a couple of years ago, and it's getting on now that it's about forty-two years old, but it's still in good condition.

I bought Lillian a clock. I had never seen anything like it. When I got home, I realised the voltage was wrong. It was made for the American market, so it was rated 110 volts and not 240 volts. I bought a converter for it, and it worked fine; however, I can't remember if it ran slow or fast, as it was also reliant on the cycles of either 50 60 Hz. So, I had bought a beautiful clock to stand on the shelf but that did not work.

After the trip, I decided to leave the Merchant Navy and get a shore job.

CHAPTER 8

SHORE JOB

When I left the Merchant Navy, I had to find some other form of employment. I found a job with a scaffolding firm. It paid more money, and I loved it. The business was divided into two areas: the contract area of the business and the hiring side. I worked for the hiring side. Joe, who was a lot older than me and who had a glass eye, worked for the contract side.

My job was to ensure that all the equipment that came into the yard which needed maintenance was maintained to a high standard. This meant that any equipment's screw threads were cleaned of any debris using a wire brush then were given the slightest bit of grease with an old paintbrush so that the nut went up and down the thread easily. There could be as many as two hundred in a week to clean. There were other jobs I did as well, such as cleaning and tidying the yard.

Harry, my boss, was a caring employer. He was nearly six feet tall and had a good head of greying hair. He was of medium build and spoke softly. He always asked his employees if they minded doing something; he never ordered them to do it. This always impressed me.

Our lorry driver, now he was a character. He loved the ladies and had the charisma to charm any female. Each day he would come in and tell me what he had got up to the night before.

In those days when an employee reached eighteen, his employer had to pay him a man's wage. As I was nearing my eighteenth birthday, Harry called me into his office and told me that he would have to let me go because of this rule. He said that although he didn't want to let me go because I was a good worker, that was just how things were. He said that if I needed time off to go for an interview, I should just let him know, and I could go.

Harry asked Peter, who was in charge of the contract side of the business, if he would take me on as an apprentice scaffolder. Peter said no but gave no reason. This caused tension between him and Harry. I was surprised, as I was never late and was willing to learn.

But there always was some tension between Harry and Peter. I noticed this when I started working there. I think it might have been because Peter constantly asked Harry for equipment. On certain occasions, this left Harry short and unable to meet his customers' needs.

Harry was petrified of growing old. He never said why. I think he found it difficult to talk about. If I tried to ask him about it, he changed the subject. It was such a shame, as he was a lovely man.

I took some time off to look for another job without success. The truth is, I didn't want to leave, and I went back several times to see if there was any work going. Harry said the person who replaced me did as much good as a chocolate fireguard and that he wished he didn't have to let me go.

At one point, we had an open day at the yard for the public and prospective customers to look round. I brought my 8mm movie camera that used film and shot about four minutes of film. Nowadays, we would use a video camera.

Watching it brings back memories. I should have used more film and taken my time panning from left to right and back. At least I have a small memento of those who worked there and the building.

The scaffolding firm no longer exists, and only part of the building that is recognizable from when I was there remains on the site. Several other companies have taken over since I left and changed it.

CHAPTER 9

FILM MAKING

I eventually found employment with the Grimsby Borough Council. I did a variety of jobs including painting the white and yellow lines on the road. Working with a traffic-light company contracted to the council for installing new traffic lights.

The good thing about working for the local council at that time was they had a variety of jobs to do, and they trained workers who didn't have experience. The main thing you did need was common sense.

While at school, I had joined our local amateur dramatic society, although my acting left a lot to be desired. I auditioned for a part and didn't get it, but I was told that I could work backstage if I wanted.

I also like working with film, and before I went into the Merchant Navy, I bought an eight millimetre camera and projector. When I came out of the Merchant Navy, I thought, if I want to work in the film industry, I should look for a group or club that worked with film.

After a while, I found the Grimsby and District Cine Society. The room where the society met was down an eight foot access road, and the building had three storeys. I cannot remember what the ground floor held, but I do remember the stairs were quite steep.

Once you reached the first floor, you turned left to go into the main room. It was laid out like a professional cinema with genuine cinema seats, curtains that opened and closed, and lights that dimmed. In the projector room were controls for the lights and curtains and a large bench that could hold up to four projectors. It had everything that a large cinema had. The only difference was that instead of large thirty-five millimetre projectors, they used eight-millimetre ones.

The tea room was also used for workshops, this was on the top floor. I felt at home straight away, hooked by the fact that making films was something that I could do. Okay, maybe mine would not be as big as Twentieth Century Fox's, but at least I was on the ladder.

The camera I had was relatively basic, as was my projector. In those days, eight millimetre was silent film, and we often used a tape recorder to record the sound as we filmed.

Like on big films, mistakes do happen, and it was important to edit, or cut, these out.

Some of the workshops that the society ran were on how to edit film, not only to cut out mistakes but also to make a film more interesting.

Once you edited the film, then you needed to edit the sound. It took a long while to get the sound just right. When showing your film, you would start the film and the tape recorder and hope that they kept in synch.

Although most of the members of the society were amateurs, one man, Tony S., had worked with a professional film unit in London. This man would change my life forever and introduce me to a different world.

Tony S was about five feet seven inches tall and slim with long black hair. When talking, he was very expressive with his hands.

Tony S. had started working when he left school on Mablethorpe Beach by taking the summer trippers' photographs. He processed the film and returned to the beach a couple of hours later with the completed photographs.

Some time later, he worked in the local cinema in the projection room. However, the big city beckoned, and he was off to London. He eventually worked with a film unit promoting the company he worked for.

After several moves, he came to Grimsby to take over as manager of one of the film company's shops. The shop sold film, cameras, and projectors as well as still cameras and photographic paper.

Tony S. soon found the Cine Society and helped many members to improve their film-making techniques.

I had some questions about film-making, mainly about superimposing titles over the picture, and I was advised Tony S. was the person to ask. I found the shop where he worked and went in to ask him. Although I knew very little, I disagreed with some of his answers. He invited me to visit his flat so he could show me why what he was saying was correct.

He invited me because there wouldn't be a workshop for one or two months at the club. I knew he was very well respected for his film-making and felt privileged to be asked. I would get to watch a professional from the film industry at work.

I was to find out that filming the subject was only half the story. Tony S. often said that the way the film was edited can make all the difference in making a film a success or a failure.

Tony S. lived in a house that had been converted into three flats. Two ladies had a room each downstairs, and Tony S. occupied all of the upstairs. The house had only one bathroom, and the three tenants shared it. Each flat had its own kitchen. Although small, they were big enough for two people to work in. Tony's area upstairs included a living room, which would have been the front bedroom before conversion, that overlooked the main street. The middle room was a good-sized bedroom. The back room was about the size of a large box room, and Tony affectionately called it the den.

I rang the doorbell at 7.30 p.m. on the Thursday that had been arranged. Tony S. answered and beckoned me in. I felt at home straight away.

'Tea or coffee?' Tony S. asked.

I replied, 'Tea, please.' I gave him a rough outline of how I had become interested in film and what I hoped to achieve.

Tony answered most of the questions that I could remember to ask. Not only had he worked on a professional film unit, but had also made several full-length films on eight millimetre and won several awards.

After some discussion, Tony S. asked me if I wanted to work with him on his next film. He thought that if I saw the whole film-making process from start to finish, I would get an idea of how it was done.

Tony S. also helped many other club members on the things they thought were their weak points.

Tony S. wrote, directed, and edited most of his films. On our project, Stan was our cameraman and lighting technician, and I helped with everything else that needed to be done. Stan worked for the General Post Office (GPO), as it was called then, and was also very good with electrics. I found out that Stan worked on quite a few of the films that Tony S. had made while living in Grimsby, and they made a good team.

One film, *The Uninvited*, took around eleven months to complete. Most of the filming took place on Tuesday evenings and some weekends. The house we used, a bungalow off the beaten track, belonged to one of Tony's friends.

It was hard work because everything had to be done more or less the same way as in the big films. The only differences were that we didn't have special effects to help out or a film crew of 200 people or more.

It was an excellent time in my life. I experienced everything I wanted to know about film-making, just on a small scale.

I found it fascinating to watch Tony's next script take shape as he wrote it. Finding the right location for filming in itself was difficult, and then filming, editing, and finally showing the finished film was a big thrill, and to think, I was a part of it.

Films are shot out of sequence. In our case, all the interior shots were filmed first and the outside shots second. When the film came back from the film laboratories, it was cut up into its respective scenes of the right length, all numbered, of course.

After all the film was shot and cut, it was re-assembled in the correct sequence, and the final edit took place. We had to concentrate otherwise we could put a part in the wrong place.

The film that went through the camera was silent. Once the editing had been completed, it was then sent off to another laboratory to have a very fine piece of magnetic tape glued down one side of the film.

We recorded sound at the time of filming using a tape recorder. We transferred the audio scene by scene onto the magnetic strip in synchronisation with what was happening on the film. This is called post-production and could take a lot of time to get things just right.

The Uninvited was around twenty minutes long. Tony S. always used more film than he needed, as he use to say, you can always shorten a scene if required, but you cannot add what you haven't shot.

I loved the whole process of film-making and worked on several other films with Tony and Stan. It wasn't long before I started to write several short film scripts.

With the help of Tony S. and others at the club, I won a couple of awards. Each year we ran several competitions on set subjects. Several people would enter, and a panel of judges would pick the winner and give out the awards at the Annual Club Dinner.

Although the club was called the Grimsby and District Cine Society, they also held slide competitions.

About twice a year, other clubs came to visit us and vice versa. On occasion, the visiting club was asked to judge either the films or the slides.

As film was replaced by video, clubs such as this one went into decline until they closed or merged with other clubs. Our cine club joined forces with the Cleethorpes Camera Club.

Although forty years have passed since some of those films were made, I still have the original films as well as the projector. Around the year 2002, most of the films were converted to DVD. Unfortunately, some of the sound had gone because the glue that was used to stick the magnetic tape to the film disintegrated over time. Because we used Kodachrome film stock for both films and slides, their colour is as good today as when they were shot.

CHAPTER 10

THE EAST LINDSEY METAPHYSICAL SOCIETY

Tony S. brought up at some point that he was the principal of the East Lindsey Metaphysical Society, or ELMS. I asked him what the word 'metaphysical' meant and what the society did.

Tony S. explained that the ELMS had been set up in response to a haunting that had taking place in a house on the Nunsthorpe Estate in Grimsby. Things were being moved around, noises were heard, and other things were happening. The family were beside themselves.

Several members of the public read about what was happing in the local newspaper. One local newspaper reporter, one local newspaper photo and print technician, one medium, and one electronics technician, who eventually rigged up a closed-circuit television system and Tony S. came together to investigate.

These people were invited to the house to try to find the cause of the strange happenings. They did not have any of the sophisticated equipment that we have today. Video recorders were not yet available for the domestic market. The team had only thermometers, tape recorders, and a good ear, of course.

After several months, the family were re-housed. At no time during the investigation did the family mention wanting to move although this had been voiced by people outside of the family. The family just wanted this to stop so they could get on with their lives. When they were re-housed, the problems followed them to the new one for a short period of time. Eventually, the activity stopped.

The group had several discussions after this investigation and decided, as they all got on well together, that they would try to sort out other similar problems.

It's important in any group that the people blend together.

This was why the ELMS invited potential members to an evening session and did not take in those who turned up on the doorstep.

I was lucky. After the group had a discussion about me, they invited me to come along one Monday evening. I was apprehensive. I finished work at five and went home for my tea, and at about seven o'clock, I arrived at Tony's and pressed the doorbell.

Tony came downstairs and invited me in. As I followed him upstairs, my heart was racing. The others had already arrived and were settled in their seats. Tony S. introduced me to the members of the group that were there.

I was surprised to find that they looked like ordinary people, although I don't know what I expected them to look like. Maybe I thought the men would be in suits and the woman in evening gowns.

At seven-thirty, a tea towel was thrown around the ceiling light, as there were no dimmers in those days, to give the room a more subtle light and to create a better atmosphere. Tony S. asked for a volunteer to open in prayer, after which we sang the 'Battle Hymn of the Republic', the society's anthem, and said the Lord's Prayer. I was then officially welcomed and introduced by Tony S.

One of the members, May, nearly always brought broth, stew, or hotpot, which I must admit was fantastic. She wasn't very tall and was on the broad side with a beautiful personality. She spoke quietly and with purpose. If I remember correctly, she worked as home help. Her daughter, Melody, was also a member and was very intelligent. She was about the same size as May.

At this point, Tony S. said that we would ask for healing for those people whose names had been given. They called this 'absent healing' because the people to be healed were not there in person.

Sometimes, a picture would be placed on a small table in the middle of the room. I enjoyed this because of the past healing that I had done, and asking for others always made me feel better. Very often the people that we were asking for had no idea the group were asking for them.

Our medium, Peter, was around five feet seven inches tall and had a beard; black, slightly wavy hair; and a deep voice. On some occasions, he would take deep breaths and bow his head a little. After a short time, he would grunt and raise his head.

With a smile on his face, he said, 'Good evening, my friends,' in a voice slightly different to his own.

Everyone replied, 'Good evening.'

This was my first introduction to trance mediumship and one which I will never forget. A chill went up and down my spine, and I felt light-headed. The members' faces lit up, and it was obvious that this had happened before. I must admit, this took me by surprise.

I felt comfortable with the proceedings and at no time felt anxious. It was also my first experience of someone changing his voice. If you have not seen this before, it can be a little frightening.

Peter's voice had changed slightly to that of a Chinese person. I can't remember exactly what he said, as it was a long time ago; however, he said something to the effect that the spirit speaking through Peter had waited a long time for me and that he was pleased that my mind had finally opened up to sense him.

After a while, the spirit said through Peter that his name was Ching and that he had been my grandfather in a previous life and was to guide me through this one.

Ching went on to say many things about my life that I could relate to. It was a lot to take in for one so young, especially on the first night of visiting the group. Ching added that both my parents in my previous life had been killed and that he had taken me in. He was a monk in a closed order, and I grew up in the monastery with him and learned their ways after my parents had gone.

The picture that he painted of the monks and their lives was beautiful. He explained that it was a hard life because the monks really had to search their souls for their own truth.

That first meeting opened my eyes and helped me to understand that what I had sensed in my bedroom had been real and not some fantasy. I had many questions, but I would have to wait a very long time for some of the answers.

'If we are to understand the answer to a question, we must first understand the question,' I was told. This still holds true for me today.

I have always felt an affinity for China and the surrounding countries. I found it remarkable that someone I have never seen before was able to give me so much detail about my life. This was the first small step on a long road.

By talking to others, I found that I wasn't the only one that had asked certain questions. That first meeting opened my eyes to the endless possibilities of what can be achieved working with and for Spirit.

Everyone in ELMS took what we were doing seriously but still retained some humour. We wrote down our questions and the answers. This gave us an invaluable reference to work from.

With the information coming through so fast, we used a tape recorder and then typed the notes up later.

The members of ELMS were a great bunch of people, and some were characters. I was the youngest of the group at that time, around eighteen. The oldest I think was in their mid-sixties.

Because everyone came from a different background, we always had plenty to talk about. The haunting on the Nunsthorpe Estate brought about a renewal of interest in the paranormal, and we had to limit the number of applications for membership.

On occasion, we went out of town to investigate alleged hauntings. Tony S. had a very good filing system and recorded and catalogued nearly every evening. There were dozens of tapes that needed to be typed up for the files each week. There are now two books that were written from these notes.

Interestingly, the first three pages of the first book are the most important. These were typed up on an old-fashioned typewriter. No computers or spellcheckers in those days. If the typist wasn't sure of the spelling of a word, she looked it up in the dictionary, so the books took a long time to write, but looking back, the effort was worth it.

Our group were lucky that we had an experienced medium at nearly all meetings. This was important because someone had to be able to communicate with those in the spirit world.

There are not as many home Spiritualist groups or circles today as in years past. Development is important, as it teaches how to open and close your mind to spirit. Some people also think that in six weeks they can be the best medium or healer on the planet. Not so.

Some learn very quickly while others struggle. It doesn't matter how long it takes; I always say it will take as long as it takes. As with most activities, you improve with practise. You must remember that a medium deals with the feelings and emotions of people on both side of the veil.

It can take many years to achieve a high level of competence. The biggest lesson that I learnt was patience. When a good medium works well, he or she makes the role look easy, possibly because that person has spent many years honing the craft.

Even now I go to an awareness group on occasions at our church, as it can bring me down to earth, and it's a good refresher course.

The ELMS sat for many years asking questions of Spirit. Peter, our medium, was also what's called a trance or physical medium.

Another type is a mental medium, who will perceive thoughts from a spirit communicator and convey them to the recipient. Only the medium can hear, see, or sense the spirit communicator.

In contrast, a physical medium goes into a trance and allows the spirit to use his or her vocal cords in such a way the recipient can recognise who is speaking. The medium's facial features may change to match those of the spirit communicator. All those in the room can see the changes and hear what is being said.

Physical mediumship requires a different form of development to mental mediumship. I was to witness many evenings of trance and direct voice mediumship with Peter being the medium in the group.

On one Monday evening, things changed. We sat as usual and went through our ritual of our hymn, prayer, and absent or distant healing. Peter's head bowed. Then he grunted as usual and raised his head. After about two minutes, his face began to change from his normal colouring. His colouring changed to a pearl shade.

Soon, a pair of old-fashioned glasses that were small and round with thin wire arms appeared on his face. Peter's hair colour changed slightly through from dark black to the pearl colour, and his face underwent other small changes. Everyone in the room saw this.

I blinked several times, thinking my eyes were deceiving me, and sat in amazement. This was something the ELMS had seen before, so it was no surprise to them.

There were only a handful of occasions when these types of events would take place at our meetings.

I feel very privileged to have witnessed these events because groups such as the ELMS are few and far between today.

Strange as it may sound, I am the only working medium that has emerged from the group over the past four decades. It's sad, really, as it would have been nice to have exchanged stories over the years with others that had developed as mediums through the ELMS.

In 2012, there are only three left living from the original group: Vera, Peter (not the medium but a member that joined several years after), and myself.

We try to meet at least three times a year to catch up on what we have been doing since we last met.

Peter, not the medium did join another group when the ELMS disbanded because it had only about five members remaining. Most of the other members either passed on or left to pursue other interests.

Peter's new group had similar pursuits as the ELMS, but as far as I know, they were not as successful as the

ELMS. This group was a small group, but the members blended well as the ELMS did.

When Vera, Peter, and I meet, we discuss what Peter's group have been doing and how they are progressing to date.

CHAPTER 11

THE EAST LINDSEY METAPHYSICAL SOCIETY AND REGRESSION

The ELMS also worked with regression, a process in which a person can remember a previous life. We had thought of trying it, but until Peter our medium brought it to our attention again, we just left the idea on the shelf. It isn't something to be undertaken lightly.

Certainly, those around the subject had to know what they were doing. After some discussion, we decided to try it. Peter had all the information, and the evening was set. I was chosen as the person who would regress.

We used a method in which one person worked at my head and the other at my feet. I cannot explain the whole process for legal reasons. Beryl, worked at my feet, was also a nurse, which came in handy.

I lay on the floor, as the subject needed to be flat. The floor was solid concrete with a short-pile carpet. Peter worked at my head and Peter gave me instructions. After a short time, the floor felt like a ceiling, and I felt as if I was slowly sinking through it.

Peter's voice started to fade, and then I heard nothing. About twenty minutes later, I came round. Beryl was taking my pulse and the other members were making a fuss around me and asking if I was okay. I then asked what had happened. I was told my pulse had slowed and my temperature had dropped, and Beryl showed some concern. With this in mind, Peter asked me to come back several times, but I didn't respond.

A good cup of hot sweet tea brought me round completely, and I felt no ill effects. It was suggested that I may not be a good subject; however, I did want to go through it again.

Other subjects were chosen with varying success. We followed up on information the subjects gave and made some outstanding discoveries.

I did go through regression again. On this occasion, the group invited a local radio station to witness the event. They knew of regression but had not seen anyone go through it.

It was a very good session, and plenty of information came through, which was either recorded or written down.

There is division amongst scholars of whether a person who regresses is really going back into a past life or is just using memories of what he or she has seen and heard, even subconsciously, and then letting his or her imagination create another time and life.

After years of research, I believe that we can regress to a former life and find out who we were and how we lived. In some cases, this can give us an insight into why we are the way we are in this life and the lessons we need to learn to help us progress both physically and spiritually.

For most people, former lives are blocked. I don't think it would benefit some people to have this knowledge, as it may stop them from learning by experience that which they need to learn in this life.

Hypnosis can be used in regression. Some hypnotists claim to have had very good results using this technique as a tool for accessing this area of the mind.

Some Spiritualist churches don't like people to talk about past-life regression. I am told this is because we cannot scientifically prove it can be done. However, when checked, some of the details a person experiences in regression cannot have possibly been known to the person before.

I can only leave it to you to make up your mind whether regression is possible, and if so, to what degree.

CHAPTER 12

Private Readings

One of the ELMS's members, Derrick, was married to Sheila. They were a loving couple with several children. Sheila was mainly interested in fortune telling. When she found out that we had one experienced medium and one developing medium in the group, she asked Derrick to ask us mediums if we needed people to practise on.

I thought this would be a good idea, as it would give me some experience. Fortune telling wasn't something I had thought about or trained for; I was being groomed only for mediumship.

To give private readings, some mediums will use cards, others will use jewellery, and years ago, many mediums had crystal balls on their tables. It is often said that all these are props, and for show. If you use cards, and there are pictures on these cards, whatever type they are, these can help. The medium will interpret what they see in the picture.

People expected a fortune teller, such as one at the seaside, to be an old lady with two crystal balls. She would charge one price to use the small one and a higher price to use the large one.

I decided I wanted a crystal ball; however, I wasn't sure where to buy one. After searching, I found them at a shop in Leeds called The Sorcerer's Apprentice.

In those days, there was not as many motorways as today. Most were narrow winding through the countryside types.

It took me about two and a half hours to get there. Tony S. planned the route, and finally we arrived. Fortunately, the weather was fine, and it was a nice drive. There wasn't as much traffic on the roads then as today which helped.

The shop was situated on the corner of a row of terrace houses. It didn't look very inviting, as it was painted black. When I went through the door, it was like I had stepped into Aladdin's cave. The store stocked everything I could possible want from ceiling to floor. Just ask for what you want and it would be there, or so I thought.

I saw a dusty, two-inch crystal ball on the shelf.

'Can I help you?' the shop assistant asked.

'Yes. I'm looking for a crystal ball about four inches in diameter,' I told him.

'I'm sorry, but we had a rush on them last month and the new delivery hasn't come in yet.'

My heart sank to the floor. I was so disappointed after going all that way.

The person behind the counter was very apologetic. 'Tell you what,' he blurted out in an excited tone. 'Although it's half the size you asked for, if you want, I will let you have the one on the shelf for five pounds. It's dusty, but I will find a box to put it in, as I have no idea where the original one is. That's the best I can do, as you have come such a long way.'

'Thank you,' I said. I turned to Tony S. and told him that one would be fine. Although I would have loved a larger one, I thought there may have been a reason the larger ones had sold out. Had it been planned that I should have this one and not a larger one?

It wasn't until we were returning home that I found out the smaller ones were made of lead crystal and the larger ones usually glass. The information booklet was quite clear that a medium can see things better in lead crystal than in glass. I found this to be true some years later.

The information booklet supplied also recommended a procedure to follow: upon purchasing a new crystal ball, you must bury it in soil. This must be done without anyone else knowing and at night. After two nights, dig it up and rinse it well under clean running water. Then polish it with a clean cloth. Don't use a duster and don't use polish. Then it would be ready. Believe me, after I had rinsed and polished it, it sparkled like diamonds.

A date was arranged with Sheila, and I turned up. I understood that only two subjects would be there for me to read. Naturally, I was apprehensive about how I would get on. You need a little ego to push you forward. You just have to keep your feet firmly on the ground, and this is why it's a good idea to be able to talk to someone. I was lucky that I had Tony S. to keep my feet firmly on the ground.

I spent many hours at Sheila's home doing readings. She loved it, and so did I. I read for a lot of her friends.

Some people use ordinary playing cards while others use tarot cards. I used ordinary playing cards, as the tarot cards could frighten people, and the crystal ball. You can read books on how to read cards. Some decks come with their own instruction booklets.

I found it best to go with my feelings. Although I had read several books on the subject, they seemed too restrictive or complicated, especially for the beginner. My main method was to ask the subject to shuffle the cards, cut the deck into three, and then pick twenty-one cards from any of the three decks. That worked for me.

My advice would be to experiment and find what works for you and then to stick to it. Change can be a good rest; however, if you are thinking of changing the way you work, try the new method first on someone who doesn't mind if it doesn't work. If it doesn't, go back to the old way for a while.

It doesn't matter if you are giving private readings or working from the rostrum: personal responsibility is always important.

I was told that a fortune teller should be able to read anything, be it tea leaves, coal fires, jewellery, or anything else. One person asked me if I could read shoes. I was up for the challenge and decided to have a go.

I think the person was having me on at the time, but I looked at his shoes, which were black with a subtle pattern. They had small heels and were well polished. He tied the laces with rather large loops.

I said to him: 'You are a person that likes things in their place and believes that there is a place for everything. I think you also like a tidy house with plenty of natural light. Dress sense is important to you, naturally, depending on the event. If you are going to do a job, you will do it to the best of your ability and won't cut corners. Although money is important to you, you know it's not everything. One last thing: your mother just said from the spirit world that the move will do you good.'

I'm sure I could have come up with a lot more. I remember being surprised myself at what I did come up with. After that, I looked for other things I might be able to read. It is true that there is more if we just look.

Sometimes I think the skill comes from the way I look at things like shoes. I have always been able to read a variety of objects. I will say that you should always have a go. Until you try, you don't know what you can do.

Have you had that feeling that tells you it's the right time to leave home? I was feeling that way with the ELMS. I felt that they had taken me as far as they could. They weren't training me to be a rostrum medium or to speak in large public halls or theatres, just to be sensitive to Spirit and vibrations.

When I think about it now, I realise I was being called to service. Why or where, I had no idea. I spoke at length with Tony S. about this, but he had no idea either. As the weeks went on, the feeling got stronger. Then one day, I thought I would go to our local Spiritualist church.

They held an Open Circle on each Wednesday evening starting at seven-thirty. I spoke to Tony S. to get his thoughts on this and told him that I was thinking of taking a year off from the ELMS to see if I could find a group to help me develop further. As the next few weeks passed, I spoke to Tony S. further on the subject; after all, he had been mentoring me for quite a few years.

I didn't want the ELMS to think I was deserting them, so I decided to tell them of my plan at the next meeting. Besides, they were also my friends.

To a certain degree, it felt like I was saying goodbye forever rather than just for some time off. Once I explained how I felt, they were fully supportive. Some of the members had watched me develop over many years.

CHAPTER 13

ANOTHER
CHANGE OF JOB

In 1974, I felt like changing jobs. To be honest, my boss and I did not see eye to eye, and I had had several big arguments with him. At that time, I was driving a seven-and-a-half-ton Bedford tipper lorry for the council and loved the work taking sand, cement, and other building materials to various people working on different projects.

I had seen advertisements for conductors on the buses, and I thought, why not? I filled out the application form and was asked to attend an interview. I handed in my notice to the council.

Most bus companies were run by local housing councils at that time. The buses were in one sense a division of the council. I spent three days in the conductors' training school after which my name appeared on the general roster. Conductors worked with another conductor for route training and learning to operate different types of vehicles.

I loved conducting, and the ticket machines were easy to use. When I got use to them, I could turn out a ticket in a matter of seconds. We had no adding machines in those days, so if a conductor had, say, one and a half to wherever, he had to add the price up in his head and give the passenger the correct change.

It was only a matter of months after starting as a conductor that I was offered the chance to go on to driving school. I already had my car driving licence so it was just a case of passing my bus driving test, which I did the first time. I was lucky.

I drove buses for the next thirty-one years and loved every minute. Of course, it was shift work, which I needed to get use to, as the first bus went out at 4.40 a.m. and the last bus came in at 11.50 p.m. My shift could be anywhere within that range. If I started at 4.40 a.m., I would be finished at about 2.20 p.m. If I started at 2.10 p.m., I would finish at 11.50 p.m. One week I would be on the early turn and the next the late.

Every driver had to work some weekends. Eventually, conductors were phased out in favour of one-man operation. At this time, the council also brought in exact-fare machines, and the driver didn't handle cash at all. The public were not in favour of the exact-fare system, and after a few months, we started to give change again.

When I started this job, conductors and drivers, whichever job they were doing at the time, were respected. I worked with a great set of people, and the managers were easy to get on with. Many had worked their way through the ranks. Some drivers who were due to retire were promoted to be inspectors.

The pay was lower for a conductor than it had been for a lorry driver, but I was happier on the buses, as the crew were more like a big family. I never felt like I was going to work because of the camaraderie. It was a pleasure. Once the passengers got to know me, I made a lot of friends and could have a laugh with them.

Once I was on the main rota you could almost plan even three years ahead, as very little changed, so it was easy to accept bookings from churches for the weekends.

There were many characters on the buses. One woman called Ada looked as if she came out of the 1930s. She always had her hair up in a bun, and she wore thick red lipstick like some of the old film stars wore.

I found out that she was a medium, and by all accounts a good one. Ada was allocated as my conductress for a while. I wanted to know about someone who I was suspicious of, so I asked this person to write something down with a new pen. I then asked Ada if she would hold the pen and tell me what came through.

I was amazed at how much about the character of this person that she picked up on. She warned me that this person was not honest and would use people. She said much more, but I cannot remember the rest. I do know that what she said was correct. This would be proved over time.

Ada had had a bad twenty years before I met her. She lost one of her two sons and then her husband. Sadly, Ada died of cancer, and that was another character gone. Someone told me that she was a good pianist. I met many similar characters to Ada.

When I was conducting a bus once, the driver pulled up at a stop at Top Town Market in Grimsby, which was our timing point. I left the bus just to pop to the shop directly opposite, but when I came out, my bus wasn't there. I caught the next bus going the same way to catch up. The driver said a little boy had rung the bell and the driver thought it was me, so he left. He realised several stops further down the road that I wasn't on the bus, so he waited for me.

This caused some laughter amongst the staff. The management weren't too happy, as conductors weren't supposed to leave the vehicle except to go to the toilet, and were supposed to tell the driver if they did. Most of us broke that rule, though, just to pop in a shop.

One of our conductors was always in the office due to his attitude. He was a really nice bloke, but he said things that would get him into trouble. I will give you some examples.

One day, we were on the 9X route from Grimsby Town to Old Waltham. This route took us past the town's cemetery. Our bus was approaching the stop just after the junction that led to the cemetery itself. The conductor called out, 'Next stop, the cemetery, dead centre of town.' Not something you should say.

On a different route, as we pulled up to a bus stop, a passenger asked this conductor if we went through to Cleethorpes.

The conductor replied, 'Sorry, no.'

The passenger was quick to answer, 'But it says that you do on the timetable.'

The conductor replied sharply, 'It says India on the tyres, but we don't go there either.'

The last example is one of the classics. We had just pulled up to a multi-bus stop, where several buses serving different parts of town stopped at the same stop. The passenger asked, 'Excuse me, conductor. I've been waiting for the number 45 route bus. Can you tell me how long the next one will be?'

The conductor said, 'About forty-three feet long.'

If I remember correctly, and I'm sure I do, that was the remark that got him the sack. Conductors were taught that passengers could be your friends or your enemies. To be honest, I didn't have any problems with passengers. Of course, I had to calm some people down. On the whole, though, the passengers were great.

There are many other great stories of life on the buses. Some are like the series *On the Buses*. It was while working in this job that I decided to go to the Spiritualist church to see what it was all about. Like my first visit to the ELMS, I felt at home as soon as I walked through the doors.

Like many people walking into a church like this, I was apprehensive the first time. I had heard so many stories and, of course, had been influenced by what I saw on television. There is no need to worry. As one person said to me, 'It's the living that will hurt you, not the dead.'

I will also say that if you are thinking of going to a Spiritualist church, have an open mind. Don't judge the church by your first visit. Go several times before you make up your mind.

CHAPTER 14

CHURCH OPEN CIRCLE

I attended the Open Circle one Wednesday evening when I was on the early shift at work. During this event, the attendees all sat in a circle and several mediums gave messages to those who they felt drawn to.

Some of the mediums were experienced while others, called fledglings, had been through an awareness or development group and wished to spread their wings.

Fledglings would go to the Open Circle and give one or two short messages until they gained enough confidence to stand on the public rostrum on their own. This took time.

Anyone could attend the Open Circle and work if they wished. It was a good evening to practise what you had learnt within your awareness or development group.

It was through this group that I learnt that the church held awareness and development groups.

The next evening, I spoke to Tony S. about what had happened at the church. I decided to attend the development group, led by Tony F.

Tony F. was a nice person who encouraged all of us. In those days, development groups ran for about twelve weeks. Tony S. kept me informed of what was happening in the ELMS, and also kept the ELMS informed of my progress.

The first night I attended the development group, there were around ten of us. We were all from different backgrounds. Some had been in development groups before and others, like me, were first-timers.

Tony F. worked with a guide call Say-Loo. I don't think that's how he spelt it, but that's how he pronounced it.

Tony F., like Peter, worked in a trance. At seven-thirty, the lights were dimmed and gentle music played in the background to create a relaxing atmosphere.

Tony F. first introduced himself to the group and then went round and asked us each what our names were and what experience we had. This broke the ice, as it can be difficult for shy people to speak in public, even in a small group like this.

Tony F. then introduced himself and Say-Loo and went on to say that he would go into a light trance to allow Say-Loo to come through. He wanted to reassure us that there was nothing to worry about.

I had seen this practise before and was looking forward to it. Tony F. closed his eyes and bowed his head slightly, as Peter had done. As he raised his head about a minute later, he greeted us with, 'Good evening, my friends.'

Everyone responded, 'Good evening, Say-Loo.'

Say-Loo then went on to say that he would look at each of us to make sure we were compatible with each other, and of course, we were.

Say-Loo spoke at great length about what our spirit guides expected from us and what we could expect from them, provided we were respectful of our gifts.

At the end of the session, Say-Loo wished us well in our development, said that he would speak with us next week and left. Tony F. lowered his head. After about a minute or so, he raised his head and opened his eyes. He asked if we were all okay and whether we understood what Say-Loo had said. I think everyone did.

The weeks flew past. I attended the weekend services as often as I could, watching and listening to how speakers and demonstrators worked. Some were obviously better than others. I thought at the time how privileged they were to stand on the rostrum and communicate with Spirit for those in the congregation.

If I remember correctly, Tony F.'s group met for around thirteen weeks. We spent some of this time meditating to help us change our conscious perception in preparation for Spirit communication. Other weeks, Tony F. helped us give what we received from Spirit in a respectful, meaningful, and uplifting way and to always remember personal responsibility.

One Saturday night a couple of years on, a small old lady led the church service. She held a handkerchief in her left hand and moved very little on the rostrum. Some mediums pace up and down while taking the service. She was very confident in what she gave to the congregation.

'I'd like to come to the gentleman at the back,' she said assertively. I was at the back of the room, but I turned round to see if she was referring to someone behind me. 'There's no one behind you, young man, except the wall.' Everyone laughed.

I had seen other people turn round when they were at the back and laughed myself, and there I was, doing the same thing.

'Spirit is strong with you, and your guide tells me you should be up here.' This took me by surprise, as I had never thought of myself standing on the rostrum.

With assertiveness in my voice, I replied 'Oh, no thank you.'

'Yes you will,' she added. I could feel my cheeks turning red. I conceded at this point, as it was clear from some of the other messages that she had given that she didn't take no for an answer.

She went on to give me other information that was accurate, especially when describing members of my family who are in Spirit. From what I can remember, most of the messages that she gave during the course of her demonstration were uncannily accurate. It's now my belief that it's Spirit that chooses you and not you that chooses Spirit.

After watching this lady and other very good mediums work, I thought that I had a long way to go to come up to their standards. Just maybe Spirit was telling me that it was time to start. I also asked myself at the time whether my nerves would hold out. After all, I was normally a shy person.

Speaking from personal experience, it's impossible to give an accurate time scale of when things may happen. I think a good medium may come close; however, one should not try to give specific dates if you are forecasting the future.

I'm not sure if she visited the church again, but I can't see that she wouldn't have visited us after that night, as speakers and demonstrators serve churches for many years unless something happened.

CHAPTER 15

FIRST SERVICE

After being a member of the church for a full year, I applied to be a member of the committee at the following Annual General Meeting. I was accepted, and I loved it.

Part of my duty was to serve as a chairman for speakers once a month. To explain, three members of the Committee were on duty at each service. One would welcome people in, the second would sell raffle tickets and explain to the newcomers what happened at our services, and the third would look after the speaker when he or she arrived. This same person would be the speakers' chairperson for the evening.

This system worked well if we had enough members on the committee for there to be three on duty at any one time. At times when we didn't have enough on the committee, we could work with two, but we were pushed.

The member selling raffle tickets got to know quite a few people and, of course, realise who the regulars were.

There were several mediums that I looked up to. Martin was one of them. He was well mannered and a first-class medium. His wife was also a very warm-hearted human being. I loved them both.

For quite a while, they ran a successful bed and breakfast in Cleethorpes. Martin led the Wednesday Open Circle along with several others on a rota.

Both Martin and his wife were well liked and respected, not just for their mediumship, but also for the way they ran the bed and breakfast.

I looked up to Martin because he was down to earth and a very good Medium, and he did everything he could to help anyone. A true spiritual person in every sense of the word, he practised what he preached. When he gave a message, he was always mindful of his presentation and the subject's feelings.

Martin watched me grow in the church development group. After a year or so, he came up to me and said, 'I'm going to serve a church in Lincoln on 7 February. Would you like to come?'

I was delighted that he should offer me the chance to go with him and his wife. 'I would love to. It will be good experience to see what other churches look like,' I replied.

Martin added, with a smile on his face, 'I meant for you to take the service.' I nearly fell over. My knees definitely went weak.

I told him that I didn't think I was ready. He told me he did. After a lot of persuasion, I agreed. I had a fortnight to get my head around it.

However much time you have, I don't think you ever consider the time is right. I was working on that day, but I finished reasonably early, so I had plenty of time to go home and get ready.

On 7 February 1987, we left for Lincoln. I was nervous, but I thought that was fine, although I was asking myself many questions, like, should I have said no instead of yes?

I told Martin I had some painting to do and that I should have been doing that, so I asked him if we could turn round so I could get on with it. Everyone just laughed. Martin and his wife tried to put me at ease by saying that if they didn't think I was ready, they wouldn't have asked me to come along, and they certainly wouldn't have asked me to take the service.

Martin asked if I wanted him to sit on the rostrum with me. I said no because if he was to sit with me, I might rely on him. I did ask him if he would sit in the front row so if I had problems, I could ask him to come up and help me out.

Martin had explained that the church was in a woman's house. She was a Spiritualist who had converted the downstairs into a church and lived upstairs.

When we arrived, I was back and forth to the toilet with nerves. Then the chairperson, Sally, said, 'Jim, it's time.' I took my place on the rostrum alongside Sally. At seven o'clock, she stood up and gave everyone a warm welcome and asked the congregation to stand for the first hymn.

The hymn over, the congregation sat down. When everyone was seated, Sally said, 'May I introduce our speaker for this evening? It is Jim Cork from Grimsby.'

Everyone replied, 'Good evening, Jim.'

Sally added, 'It's Jim's first time on our rostrum, and I hope you will make him feel welcome. Jim, may I ask if you would open our service in prayer?'

I stood up and said the shortest prayer I could think of. I sat down, and Sally stood up again and asked everyone to stand for the second hymn.

As we were approaching the last verse, my heart was pounding. Once everyone had sat down, Sally explained to the congregation that this was the part of the service where the medium would demonstrate his gift of mediumship and that if I came to them, they should just answer with a yes or a no.

My nerves really kicked in at this stage. All I wanted to do was run. The church itself was like so many terrace houses, although it had been converted into a small church. The centre wall had been between the front sitting room and the next room taken out. This made for a lovely warm church.

This was the first and last time I served this church, as the lady who owned it died and her family wanted the house back. Those who ran church moved into a conventional church building and hired a room for their Spiritualist meetings.

When I stood up, I looked for the person I felt drawn to for the first message. It was like someone had dimmed all the lights except for a spotlight over this person.

'Can I come to you, please?' I said as I stretched out my hand and pointed. 'I have a person here who tells me they passed over due to a stroke, and it must have affected her voice because I feel that I am struggling to get my words out. She also wants to say that in some way, around you, you also feel that you cannot say what you would like to. Can you understand who this person is?' I asked.

'Yes, I can. She has just recently passed over,' the person replied excitedly. I then went on to describe the spirit's height and character, which the recipient of the message accepted.

I was relieved and saddened at the same time, as I could feel the pain of the loss of this person's mother, as it turned out to be. It was a tremendous boost to my confidence that the first message was a good one for the person.

'She is also talking about a move, which I feel will be good for her. She is also telling me about new life that is coming to the earth plane. Does this make sense?' I said.

'Yes, it does. Some of it I can relate to someone else, but I know where it is,' the subject said eagerly.

Saturday evening services usually lasted about an hour in total. That included the welcome by the chairperson, the first hymn followed by the opening prayer, the second hymn, the demonstration by the speaker, the closing hymn, closing prayer, and finally the notices.

The last message of the evening was to a lady on my left. I remember this as if it were yesterday. She was small with a lovely head of black hair and in her mid-sixties. I looked at her several times throughout the service. The lights hadn't dimmed around her, so felt that Spirit hadn't wanted me to go to her in the beginning.

However, when Sally caught my attention and told me that I could only give one more message, as it was getting near the end of the service, I looked around the room and gave this lady another glance. The lights around her started to dim, and I knew then I was with her.

It would be nice if I could remember the entire message, but I can't. The one part of the message that has stuck in my mind is this: 'There is a gentleman in Spirit that is a relative tied to you. He passed due to a chest complaint which feels like a heart attack; however, he is telling me there were quite a few things wrong with him. I think his name was George. Can you understand this man?' I asked.

'Yes,' she replied, nearly jumping out of her seat.

'George is saying that he has the child with him. You know, the one that was lost so many years ago. George is not telling me if this child belonged to you, but if so, please get rid of the guilt for whoever this is for, they must not blame themselves. There was nothing you or they could have done.'

At this point, a lump came to my throat. I was so emotional and full of passion. 'I'm sorry, he's leaving. Bless you. Thank you ladies and gentlemen, for letting me work on your rostrum and blend with your loved ones.' I then sat down, and seconds later, Sally stood up and thanked me for the service. Then she asked if everyone would sing the last hymn of the evening while seated while the steward came round to collect the free-will offering.

It was difficult for me at that point, as my mind kept drifting in and out of the messages that I had given. Sally then asked me to close in prayer, after which we all sang 'Lord, Keep Us Safe This Night'.

When I came off the rostrum, I walked into things and couldn't get my bearings. Martin explained that this can happen when a medium goes deep while giving messages. He also explained that it would wear off and that it was best just to sit on my own for a few minutes while I came back.

While having a cup of tea afterwards, I asked Martin if I did okay. He told me that I had done better than some mediums who had been working on the rostrum for the past twenty years. *Wow*, I thought, and in my mind, I thanked Spirit not just for the opportunity but also for those who gave me the information to pass on.

I spoke at length with Martin on the way home, and I asked him, 'Where do I go from here?' This is always a difficult question to ask anyone.

'I'm not you, and only you can know where you want to go,' Martin explained. 'Now you have done your first service, other services will come in. As time goes on, you will gain in confidence.' He said this with some excitement in his voice. I also spoke to Tony S. shortly afterwards and learnt he was surprised by how well I had done on my first engagement.

After some discussion, Tony S. agreed to be my manager, taking all the bookings and so on. We also agreed that he wouldn't take any money for what he was doing, adding that he was only too pleased to be helping in some way.

After being told of the evening at Lincoln, the ELMS members were delighted that it had gone well.

They asked me if I had any more bookings. I told them that Sally had given me another date but that it wouldn't be at that church, as it was closing. Sally telephoned soon after to tell me where the congregation would meet in the future.

It wasn't long before my name was going around and the telephone calls came in for me to serve other churches. I was delighted. The more I stood on the rostrum, the more I loved it.

There is never any guarantee that events will go according to plan. You have to trust in Spirit and work as a medium for the right reasons. Very often even now I'm not sure if I will be able to work on the night until I make that first link. Spirit never lets us down. It's us that lets Spirit down.

It's often said that at times, Spirit switches you off if for health conditions or if you need a break, or if you need to be taught a lesson. Let me give you one example of this.

I received a telephone call from one church that I hadn't worked before. It was a nice-sized main hall for about fifty congregants and was full. The chairperson introduced me, and we got off to a fine start.

As usual, there was good evidence and gentle humour. I enjoyed the service and was soon given several other bookings. I was over the moon that I was able to blend with family and friends from the spirit world for the congregation.

Several months later, I returned. People were being turned away, as the church was full. It's always sad when this happens, as sometimes people have travelled many miles to attend.

As before, the chairperson gave me a warm welcome followed by the first hymn. I opened in prayer, and then we sang our second hymn, an uplifting one, which helped lift the vibrations.

The chairperson then stood up and told the congregation that I would now demonstrate my gift of mediumship and added that if I got to a person, that person should just answer yes or no.

I then stood up and looked for my first link. I didn't see lights go dim around anyone.

Just before I was going to go to a person, it was like a gust of wind passed me and went out the door. After that, the atmosphere was silent.

I wasn't sure what was happening or why. I stood there for what seemed to be ages and then just took pot luck. The first person I went to said no to most of what I said, and so did the second and third. My confidence was going downhill fast.

There was nothing more I could do. I just had to be honest and admit that I wasn't able to work. I said, 'Ladies and Gentleman, for whatever reason, I don't have anything. It's as if all the energy has gone out of the room.'

A small voice from the second row said, 'I felt it as well. There was a gust of wind that passed you and then me, and then nothing. Silence.' We spent the rest of the evening with a question-and-answer session. It happened to turn out to be a very good night, even though there was no mediumship as such.

Several members of the congregation came up to me afterwards and said that at least I was honest and for that I had earned their respect.

It taught me a valuable lesson: never take for granted what Spirit has given you. Mediums are blessed with a beautiful gift. They should never take it for granted, as what is given can be taken away.

In conversation with other mediums, most have said that a similar event hasn't happened to them. Only one or two I asked admitted that they too have stood on the rostrum and have been unable to work for whatever reason.

I've always said that you can never guarantee that anything is going to come through. We must trust in Spirit. It is always best to be honest than to try to fool people. To gain respect, you have to give respect.

I've been in congregations when speakers could not work and watched them fall from grace because they said anything but the truth.

CHAPTER 16

ON THE ROAD

I n the early days of my mediumship, the roads weren't as good as they are now. Grimsby is on the east coast, and many churches that I was booked to serve were many miles away. Although I loved driving buses, it was a pleasure to drive the car long distances.

Some of the churches I went to were down long, narrow roads, and I needed to allow plenty of time to have a cup of tea before the start of the service.

Most of the churches at that time had either a piano or organ. I always took some sheet music with me so I could play for about half an hour before the start of the service as people filtered in. Sometimes if I was serving a church that held two services, one in the afternoon and the other at night, I would spend about an hour in between playing hymns.

Unfortunately, most of those who played regularly at these churches have passed on, and no one seems to want to play nowadays. I think it's because it requires a commitment to go to church at least twice a week.

On quite a few occasions, I would drive buses for eight hours, change into my suit in the locker room, and then go off to a church, eating one or two sandwiches when I arrived. On most occasions, Tony S. would go with me. He was brilliant at navigating. He would study the map at least two days before we went anywhere. This would give him time to look for the shortest or best route to get there. There was no satnav in those days; we had to rely on good old-fashioned map reading.

I sometimes travelled to a church to work in their Open Circle. After working in one of these, the person leading the circle would ask if I was a medium and if I was working the church circuit, and I would give that person my telephone number. Several weeks later, that church's speaker's secretary would phone to ask if I had any spare dates for a booking.

Some churches liked to see a medium work before making a booking rather than take someone else's word for it. I think this was better for me, as I could take my time finding the church. Several were off the beaten track, so it did take some time to find them.

Within about six months, Tony S. had booked me at churches for the next two years. We didn't have many Saturdays or Sundays free, as we travelled to serve a church when I wasn't at work.

Most of the churches were full, and standing room only on many occasions. It was always nice to work to a full church, as it lifted the vibrations. I also like to work with gentle and natural humour. After all, communicating with your loved ones should be joyous, not morbid or too serious.

If a church was very far from Grimsby, sometimes they would ask if I wanted to take several private sittings to offset the petrol cost. Occasionally I would say yes. I did have to be a little careful, as this work could be tiring and can make for a very long day.

For example, once I drove nearly three hours, took four private sittings, then went on the rostrum for ninety minutes, and then made the three-hour journey back.

When you're young, you may not think anything of it, but as you get older, you tend to slow down, so it is important to think about these things before saying yes.

CHAPTER 17

CONTENT OF INFORMATION

There are many things Spirit will give you to relay to a recipient. A medium must remember personal responsibility. This means that he should think about what he's saying and how he's going to say it. You want people to leave feeling uplifted, not feeling more depressed than when they first came in.

Sometimes it's not easy to do. You don't know what people have been through. They may have just lost someone and are emotional and vulnerable.

Some mediums say that you should not interpret what Spirit gives you. However, sometimes you need to do that to put over what you are given without upsetting the person or persons the message is for.

This is a skill that comes with experience; however, a development group should teach it. It's so easy to talk fast and give everything Spirit gives to you, but if you are not thinking about what you are given and allow it to just come out, this could create problems.

For example, I was serving a church many years ago when I found it difficult to work. It was as if I was just off tune and missing some important information. I told the congregation that I needed a minute to sort things out.

Then I knew where I wanted to be. 'Can I come to you, please?' I asked, pointing to a woman about halfway down on my right.

'Bless you,' she said excitedly.

I could see a man clearly in my mind's eye. I then said to the woman, 'I see a man who is about five feet tall, has dark hair, and is about my build. He had a nice character when he was on the earth plane but wouldn't have suffered fools gladly.'

The woman's eyes lit up, and she moved forward in her seat slightly.

'Can you understand who this man is?' I asked.

'Oh yes,' she replied.

This is where personal responsibility came in. I could see him walking through overgrown grass into the distance. A glint of light reflected off his shoes as he waded through the grass. It became evident that he was walking through a flooded field.

'He is walking through some longish grass, and there looks to be some standing water. I think he must have tripped, because he is falling down. It also looks as if he hit his head when he fell. I can now see blood from what looks like a head wound. Can you understand this?' I enquired.

'Yes, I can,' the woman said, her voice faltering slightly.

The next part gave me reason for concern. 'Something is not quite right here. I'm having a little difficulty. Please bear with me,' I said.

Another man passed me in the scene, went up to the first man, and struck him on the head with a rock. Then he calmly walked off. How on earth was I going to say this? Should I leave that bit out?

If I told her everything that I had seen, would it spark a police investigation? I thought of playing it safe. 'Like I said before, something is not quite right. It seems as if this man was not alone. Can you understand this part?'

Her reply was swift. 'Yes, I can. It's been going on for quite a period of time and causing problems within the family.'

I trusted Spirit and thought, *I'm sure Spirit will support me through this.* Mediums must be careful not to cause any more distress than a person already feels. This was not the first time this kind of information had come through.

I wasn't sure how to proceed at this point, as the woman was clearly looking for answers. I pulled on all of my experience to deal with this message as diplomatically as possible.

The woman then added, 'The investigation suggested that he was not alone, and this is proving it.' I could hear the expectation from the congregation, as some of them knew the story. 'There was some doubt that the fall caused the injury to his head. Although investigators found a large stone with blood on it, they said he hit his head on this when he fell. The question is, how did he trip and fall in the first place?'

I thought this would be a good place to break the link. I must admit, the room was absolutely silent as I received the message from Spirit. I have been back to serve that church again. I don't remember who the woman was, and no one has said anything to me since in relation to that message.

Suicides can be another distressing link. One church I went to many years ago was full. I had been given several messages, but the evening wasn't going too well. I knew something was wrong but I couldn't put my finger on it.

Sometimes, I just knew instinctively when I said the opening prayer that someone was waiting in the wings, as it were, to come through. Spirit will give you cues, and when I stumbles saying the opening prayer at this service, I took it as my cue. The question was, should I let this message come through first or last?

'I'm going to stop the service for a minute, as something is not quite right,' I said assertively. I looked at a woman in the second row and four seats to my right. 'May I come to you, please?' I asked.

'Bless you,' she said.

'I have a gentleman with me. He is about my build with dark eyes and dark hair. He was wearing light blue jeans, a jumper, and a dark jacket. My head feels like it won't switch off. There is so much going on. He tells me he took his own life?' Straight away I felt I had the right connection. 'You have been struggling with this for a number of years. I feel as if I am struggling to get my breath. Can you understand this?' I asked, leaning towards the woman from the rostrum.

'Yes I can. He hanged himself,' she replied.

I stood there in silence for what seemed to be minutes, but I'm sure it was seconds. 'I wasn't told what he used to take himself over. What I can say is he's fine but concerned about you. I want to say, and I always say this, please get rid of the guilt. There was nothing that you or anyone else could have done. He had problems and felt that he could not talk to anyone. He says that he is sorry for the people that he's left behind, especially the little one.'

This she confirmed. I gave her more information about him, and when she started to cry, a lump came to my throat which I had trouble controlling.

More often than not, when I start the opening prayer and stumble, it's because a suicide is waiting in the wings to come through. Emotionally, it's not easy to bring suicides through, as they can be draining, but having said that, they can also bring relief to those family members who are looking for some form of closure.

Over a cup of tea after the service, the woman told me that she had been waiting thirty years for someone to tell her that there was nothing that she could have done to prevent this man taking his own life. It seemed that no one thought of her suffering in this way because she was not a direct family member; however, she was very close to him, almost like a sister.

Most speaker's secretaries I'm sure would like to see a medium work before booking him or her on the rostrum. I think this is because so many older mediums have either retired or passed on. Some speaker's secretaries have been booking those just coming out of awareness or development groups a little too early, possibly without them going on the rostrum with a experienced medium a few times first.

Those mediums who teach development groups say that you as the medium should give to the recipient what you receive. This is not always a good idea, as the information could frighten the person or make the person more depressed. This is where personal responsibility comes into play, as I mentioned before.

There is a difference between church rostrum mediumship and private readings. When I'm on the rostrum, I'm always aware that other people are in the room and maintain personal responsibility knowing that. I try not to open things up too much and to keep to evidential mediumship. It's a case of judging each message as it come in and giving accordingly.

When you are giving someone a private reading, however, often just you and the recipient are in the room. This allows you to go into more depth and to be more personal. Also, I think recipients are more responsive, as they aren't as worried about what comes forward, as what is said is confidential.

I was driving a bus on a late shift one evening, and I only had to go from Grimsby Town through to Cleethorpes and then to the depot before I was finished. I had probably less than one hour left.

My friend Sheila was waiting at one of the bus stops not too far from where she lived. 'What are you doing when you finish work, Jim?' she said with a little concern in her voice after I opened the doors.

'Going home and then to bed. Where else would I go at nearly twelve midnight?'

Sheila then explained that Madge, a medium friend of ours, had contacted her and told her about a family worried about a young diabetic man. He had left the pub but no one could find him.

Although it was very late, I couldn't just leave it. 'I'll be round to yours as soon as I finish. I think it will be about half past twelve.'

Sheila thanked me and then headed home.

I arrived at Sheila's, and several people, including Madge, were already there. I was introduced to some members of the young man's family by Sheila. 'This is a photo of him, Jim. Can you pick anything up?' Sheila said.

I felt that there had been an argument. 'Who did this man have an argument with?'

There was no reply.

'If we are to work on your behalf, we must know the truth,' I said with assertiveness.

One of the family members owned up. He told me he had a big argument with the missing man and then stormed off. I was also told by one of the other family members the missing man had been drinking, and quite a lot.

When I looked at the photograph again, the young man was fading slightly in and out. I had seen this before; if the person had died, his or her photographic image faded partially. Madge looked at me, and I turned to look at her. I just moved my head side to side gently enough to let Madge know, I didn't think there was any hope. I felt an empty feeling in my stomach. It's a terrible feeling knowing a person has died and the other people in the room hope he is all right. Fortunately, this doesn't happen often, but when it does, it can affect me for several days afterwards.

Shelia, Madge, and I followed the trail from the pub where the man and his relative had been drinking to Chapman's Pond. This was an area of grassland and a large pond. After looking around, we then picked up a trail over the railways lines which led to the beach.

Our initial thoughts were that due to his condition, he wouldn't have been thinking rationally and may have wondered into the sea. After an hour or so, we lost the trail completely. All three of us were disheartened that we couldn't find him, and our hearts sank as we feared the worst.

Not wanting to give the family false hope, we just admitted that we had lost the trail. Two or three days later, his body was found. This devastated the family and the three of us.

I learnt many lessons from that experience, as I did from the next one. Peter, resident medium in the ELMS, was watching a news bulletin regarding a lost child on television.

One Monday, shortly after the bulletin, we sat as usual at seven-thirty. Peter's head bowed, and about a minute later, it raised, We bantered a bit with the Spirit communicator, and then we broached the subject of the missing child, with some details coming through.

At the end of the Monday sitting, Peter told us that a lot of information about the child came through while he and his wife communicated with his guide at their own home, and he gave some good descriptions to the ELMS. He went on to say that a scarf had been found near where the child was last seen which he believed had been left out of any reports.

Peter gave this information and more to the police. They confirmed that they had found a scarf and asked him how he had learnt this, as it had not been given to the public. Peter had some explaining to do. As I am sure you can appreciate, if a person gives the police details about a case that had not been made common knowledge, the Police would question that person, which was what they did with Peter.

Because Peter and his wife were members of the ELMS, everyone affiliated with that group was under suspicion to a certain degree. This was because of the amount of accurate information that Peter gave to the police.

The police knew someone who occasionally visited the ELMS who had been on the police force not long after I joined that group. This didn't concern us. Everything we did was to help other people. As this person visited the ELMS, he could see this for himself, and I'm sure he reported it to the police. The information Peter gave to the police, I believe did help.

CHAPTER 18

CHANGE OF
PERCEPTION
(REMOTE VIEWING)

Tony S. received a telephone call to ask if I could demonstrate my gift of mediumship at a large psychic centre, and I agreed. Four people had pooled all their savings to build this large house and centre with several big rooms for conferences, several small rooms for workshops, and one large room for demonstrations.

Outside at the back was a very large beautiful garden area. Several trees and plenty of seating added to its beauty. I must admit, the centre was difficult to find at first, as it was in quite a secluded area.

The service started at seven-thirty, as most meetings do. Much to my surprise, especially as it was my first time there, the room was almost full.

The first three messages I gave were very good. I provided good evidence and, as always in my services, gentle humour. The next message took me and the congregation by surprise.

I looked around for my next link and stopped around the centre of the room. I saw a woman of five feet four or five feet five. 'Can I come to you, please?' I asked.

'Bless you,' she replied.

'George wishes for you to remember him, and he's telling me that you still miss him after all these years.'

She gave me a big smile.

'Can you understand this man?' I enquired.

'Oh yes, bless him . . . It's my dad.'

At that point, the room started to change. I seemed to be standing in a bedroom far away from the stage I was on. 'I'm going to describe a room to you. Please bear with me as I get my bearings. The wall in front of me has one window with net curtains covered with darkish main curtains. There is a small dresser in front where one would put make-up on. On my left there is a wardrobe.' Then something wonderful happened.

While describing this wardrobe on my left and looking slightly in that direction, I heard a door open on my right. I turned and saw a woman of around five feet seven inches tall. She had long dark hair brushed back and tied with an elastic band and, was wearing a dark patterned dress.

'Who are you?' she asked aggressively, taking one step towards me. 'What are you doing in my bedroom?'

'Your bedroom?' I replied.

'Yes, mine,' she answered.

'I'm describing the room to the lady whom I'm giving the message to.'

Her response was quick. 'Well, I don't take kindly to strangers in my bedroom. This room is private to my husband and me.'

'I'm sorry. I'm just describing this room so the woman knows who the room belongs to.'

Then I realised I needed to explain what was happening to the congregation. I turned to the congregation and explained that I saw a woman come into the room and that she was asking what I was doing there. This was the first time this had happened when I was on the public rostrum. It was like being in two worlds at the same time. You have to experience this to understand just how strange it was.

Remote viewing is seeing places, people, or objects at a distance. They can be in this time or another time in the past or future. This technique was used during the cold war. It is alleged that the CIA and others used it to spy on their enemies, as *Psychic Warrior* by David Morehouse describes.

The book gives a fascinating insight into how remote viewing was used and how it can be used today. As well, it offers information about courses for developing this ability. Several companies advertise the services of remote viewers for hire.

For around twenty years, the program was a closely guarded secret and went under different code names:

Grill Flame, Center Lane, Sun Streak, and later on, Stargate, which has no relation to the film.

According to the book, *Psychic Warrior,* highly trained Defence Department remote viewers were used in pursuit of political military espionage targets. Morehouse was one of the first remote viewers to break ranks and expose the truth to the world.

Remote-viewing courses are not to be taken lightly. Morehouse describes that several people within the military suffered severe breakdowns due to the emotional demands of what they witnessed while in this altered state.

On a TV programme I saw one night just by accident, I saw this demonstrated. The programme featured several items including this one. It showed a live demonstration of remote viewing. Without knowing it, I was demonstrating remote viewing on the rostrum by describing streets and houses and what was inside them.

Maybe around two years later, I saw a documentary on this subject that showed several of the people who set the protocols, forms, and safety features required to ensure a good session with excellent results.

I was fascinated and soon on the Internet looking for courses on this subject. As mentioned before, several companies offered to teach the method. I sent an email requesting course material. Nearly all those offering such courses were in the United States at that time. I wasn't expecting the amount of paperwork that I received. It looked like there was enough to take a full degree.

As I did working on the church rostrum, I loved the course. I soon put some of the principles into practise.

They enhanced the way I worked and also improved my mediumship.

On one occasion, I received a telephone call from a medium, Shirley, who asked me if I was free on a certain date. I told her I was, and she invited me to work with her and another medium.

The venue was a pavilion which held several hundred people. I had not been there before, and it was a push to arrive for the start time, as I was working on that date.

We couldn't find the venue straight away, and we arrived about ten minutes late. The demonstration had already started, and Tony S. and I crept in. Peggy, one of the mediums, saw me at the back of the hall.

While Shirley, was giving a message, Peggy came off the stage, took my hand, and led me back onto the stage. I looked out at the audience and thought, *Oh my word. All these people! Where on earth do I start?*

It had been decided before I arrived that Shirley would go first, then Peggy, and then me. Both Shirley and Peggy gave some excellent messages. They were far more experienced than I was, which you might think gave me the disadvantage. Not the case.

I stood up and said, 'Good evening. My apologies for being late. I got lost, as this is the first time I have been here.' I looked around and waited for the lights to dim and highlight the person I need to be with. This didn't happen.

I looked around the room once more, and the light seemed to be brighter around one person. 'Can I come to you, please? The lady in the cream-coloured coat.'

Her answer was quite simple. 'Yes.'

The message was brief but good. 'I see a stone-walled house with a small living room and kitchen, open-grate fireplace, and simple furniture. Also, I feel that it is not in the town where we are but deeper in the Yorkshire region, but I can't be more precise at this time. The woman that lived there would have passed in her eighties. She was short and slightly built. Her husband was taller and bigger in the body. He spoke straight to the point and worked hard at manual labour, as the palm of his hands were rough. What this refers to is that he was a manual worker. Can you understand all this, please?' I asked.

'Definitely,' she said very firmly.

The other messages were similar in the way I presented them. Before I knew it, my time was up. I sat down while the chairperson for the evening thanked us. Shirley and Peggy both gave me a hug and thanked us for coming.

This evening gave me the chance to work at seven other churches because there were several speaker's secretaries in the audience. They came up to me afterwards and asked for my telephone number for bookings. This was the first time that I had worked at any venue bigger than a church. I think the maximum attendance in the biggest church that I have worked is around sixty people.

Working at more churches gave me the experience I needed to improve and progress. My communication with the spirit world went from strength to strength. I always say to any congregation that I can be wrong. Communication is not a precise science.

On television programmes that demonstrate mediumship or channelling, the demonstrators always get things right. The recipient very rarely says no. This is because the nos or I'm not sures can be edited out.

People who have seen a medium live after seeing that person on television often say to me that they didn't think the medium was as good in person. Never be afraid to say no to a medium. The medium should not think that he or she is always right.

Honesty is always the best policy. You can lose all the respect that you have built up over the years in just a few minutes if you're not honest.

CHAPTER 19

DIFFERENT WAY OF WORKING

T ony S. took a call from a church asking me if I did anything apart from straightforward mediumship. The church wanted me to do a special, where members of the congregation pay to come in rather than giving a free-will offering at the end of the service.

That evening, Tony S. told me about the call. I telephoned the church the next day and explained that if they wanted to, I would take a flower service. They agreed, and we set a date for about one month ahead.

That night I told Tony S. about the service. He asked me what it entailed, and I explained that the congregation are told in advance to pick and bring a flower from their own garden; it didn't matter whether the flower was just a weed.

When they arrive at the church, they secure one part of a raffle ticket around the base of the flower, and they keep the other part. The flowers are collected on a tray.

The chairperson tells the congregation at the start of the service that the demonstrator will pick up one of the flowers from the tray, and read the number out. The congregants must not tell the demonstrator who the flower belongs to until the demonstrator asks who the number belongs to at the end of the reading, which will be a character reading.

'I'm not going with you on that night,' Tony S. said.

'Why not?' I asked.

'You've never done it before. I don't want to see you fall flat on your face,' he replied.

'I've seen it done, and I think I can do it,' I told him with some excitement in my voice. I finally convinced him to go. We arrived in plenty of time. I sat out of the way so I couldn't see which flowers or weeds which people were bringing in. Tony S. sat in the main hall of the church as people came in.

At seven-thirty, the chairperson stood up and gave everyone a warm welcome. After the first hymn, I was invited to open the service in prayer. The chairperson then handed the service over to me.

'Good evening. The idea for tonight is for me to pick one of the flowers from the tray and call out the number; please do not tell me if you have that number until the end of the reading. Once I pick the number, I will then read the character of the person who brought the flower from the colours and texture of the flower. When I have finished, I will ask who has the number that has been fixed to the bottom of the flower and how accurate the reading was.'

I picked up the first flower and called out the number.

The chairperson said, 'Oh, that's mine.' Everyone laughed.

'That's that one out the window,' I replied. 'Shall we start again?' I turned towards the tray and picked up the next flower. 'This is number forty-two. If you notice, there are two main flowers and two buds. This can indicate that there are four in the family, two adults and two children. However, as one of the buds has almost died, this could indicate that one of the children has gone back to Spirit. The green foliage indicates that this person has strong roots, I think, and is very family orientated. They have their feet very firmly on the ground. As one of the main flowers has yet to fully open, this may indicate that there is a lot more for this person to do both physical and spiritually. Another flower has been added to the main one. This tells me there has been a break in family ties, that this person is divorced. Who has number forty-two?' I looked around the room.

Then a woman said, 'I do.'

Turning to the woman, I asked, 'What percentage of what I have said can you accept?'

With a smile on her face, the woman replied, 'About seventy-five to eighty-five percent.' I couldn't have been more pleased.

I picked up another flower. It wasn't very big but it felt full of character. If I remember correctly, it was a single flower. There was quite a lot of foliage at the bottom. 'The number of this one is forty-nine. I feel this person has been on their own for quite some time. They like their own space and do a lot on their own. They also take pride in their work. This person is a lover of music, and when they listen, they like to hear a piece all the way through without disturbances.' I said quite a bit more, but I can't remember the rest. 'Who has number forty-nine?' I concluded loudly.

'I do,' a man replied.

'How much can you accept?' I asked.

'Hardly anything,' he said.

This took me aback a little. All the other character readings had gone well. I took a minute to look around the room. 'You didn't pick this flower, did you?' I enquired.

'No. I came in a little late and didn't realise it was a flower service. The chairperson gave me one out of the vase.'

Turning to the chairperson, I said, 'Can you accept everything I have said?' She agreed.

This happened every time people didn't pick the flowers they brought themselves. Even if they did pick the flowers but from another garden, the reading is for the person who owns the garden, and not the person who brought the flower.

The other nine messages over the next ninety minutes followed the same pattern, although some were more detailed than others. The interesting thing is that when I spoke to the chairperson afterwards, she told me that other mediums who worked in the same way only gave three or four messages. One speaker gave only three in over an hour and a half.

I love flower services because I don't know who the person is until the end of the reading. Sometimes I'm as surprised as the recipient of the message.

Someone once told me that because I hold the flower, I read the vibrations of the person who brought it. Just to prove it still worked if I didn't touch the flower, I tried leaving the flowers on the tray, and my readings were still accurate.

When I have taken workshops, as the teacher, I have included a flower reading just to show that a medium doesn't have to be special to read flowers. He or she just has to interpret the colours and the way the buds or flowers lie.

I think I'm very lucky in that I can give character readings from flowers, shoes, tea leaves, coal fires, or other objects. It surprises me how many people are accurate when they try to give such readings. I'm sure it surprises them as well, especially when these people have told me that they couldn't do it.

Experimenting is the best way to find out your skills. Try it out on supportive friends first and then move up a gear when you have gained confidence. Like me, you won't get it right every time. There is nothing wrong with being wrong. It just makes you work harder the next time.

You may also find that when you start, the information just floods in. I always say just go with the flow.

One of my friends asked me if she could try an experiment with me. The idea was for a person to tick boxes in a form selecting flowers types, such as tulip, daffodil, rose, and flower characteristics such as colour and size and open or closed buds.

A number is written on one of the corners of the form, and then the form placed face down on a tray.

The person takes a ticket with a matching number. Just before the service starts, the tray is brought to the front.

Denise, an artist who works with me, picks up one of the forms and paints the flower the person has chosen on a large flip chart facing the congregation so the congregation can see what Denise is painting. I then read the character of the person from Denise's painting. When I have finished, then and only then will I ask who has that number. This should work very similarly to the congregation picking and bringing flowers from their own gardens. We decided to try this out.

Denise was very quick at painting the flowers, which gave me time to add a small spiritual message at the end of each character reading. Usually by the time I finished reading one, Denise started painting the next.

This was a wonderful way of working because I didn't know who the paper belonged to until the end.

Denise and I have worked this way for many years, and to date, we have only work this way together, although other mediums have asked Denise if she would work with them. It may not feel comfortable for her to work with someone new after all this time.

The other thing that I must add is that Denise and I only give these demonstrations if all the money that nights goes to a charity. I am pleased to say that many churches are happy to oblige.

Denise and I work very well together, and we engage in plenty of banter throughout the service.

As far as I know, we are the only ones to work in this way. Usually, there is standing room only at the church on these nights.

Denise will admit that she is not an artist in the true sense of the word, however, for not being trained, I think she does very well, and so do the congregants, and that's all that matters.

Once a reading has finished, a member of the committee will give the picture to the person who received the reading.

It's also interesting that I often need to ask Denise what colour a flower is. I can see colours, but do have difficulty identifying some colours. I rather think of it as colour shift. It brings some laughter to the congregation when I ask Denise what colour the flower she has painted is.

It can be frustrating to look at a colour and be unable to identify it. I've had to adjust to it. It only causes problems for me during colour services. Of course, this condition affects other areas of my life. I can work round it sometimes but not in others.

CHAPTER 20

LIFE CHANGE

In 2004 a chain of events changed my life yet again. These events stopped me working as a bus driver, caused me to be a recluse for a period of time, and stopped me working as a medium.

I was about to leave Immingham Docks on the number 45 route to Cleethorpes. I must have blacked out, and I came round near a main junction and not knowing where I was. I didn't recognise any of the roads, and I wasn't sure which road I was to take when I approached this junction.

All I remember is coming out of this blackness. I brought the bus to an abrupt stop. Shaking slightly and scared, I waited about a minute. I radioed traffic control to find out where I was.

Traffic control expressed some concern as to what had happened. Slowly, I regained my bearings and carried on. I had no idea how I had gotten from Immingham Docks to the big junction about half a mile away.

This had happened before, but I wasn't disoriented for as long or as confused after coming out of the blackness. When I returned to the depot, I just passed it off as being tired and what they call driving on automatic pilot. Control accepted this and didn't report the incident.

I was due to go for my five-year medical examination which is compulsory after the age of forty-five.

I received my papers and the date. I read the questionnaire I was to fill out very carefully. One question on page 2 asked, 'In the last five years, have you suffered from any loss of awareness?'

I went over and over this question in my mind. I knew that if I answered yes, I would lose my driving licences for a bus and a car. But if I didn't say yes, I wondered whether these episodes could get worse and what the consequences could be.

As I was driving the bus back to Grimsby town centre for my break on the morning of the exam, I thought, *This could be the last time I ever drive a bus. Do I want to risk it by saying yes to the question?* After my break, I went to the doctor's for the exam.

The doctor asked me the questions on page 1, which I had no trouble with. 'Page 2 now, Jim,' he said. He read the second question. 'In the last five years, have you suffered from any loss of awareness?' He looked directly at me.

'Can we talk about this?' I asked.

'No, it's a straightforward question,' he replied.

'I need to talk about this to understand what loss of awareness is.'

The doctor smiled slightly and quickly replied, 'You just need to answer yes or no.'

I said, 'Yes.'

The doctor told me he would have to suspend me from work. He telephoned my employer and informed him of his decision and the reasons behind it. He said that my licence would be suspended pending a medical investigation and advised me to visit my own GP.

The doctor then closed the questionnaire and asked me what had happened. I explained all my symptoms, past and present. He went on to say that I had a responsibility to my passengers as well as myself. I told him that was why I had said yes to the question, even though I knew I would be suspended.

I went on to tell him that I was having several episodes a week in which I would lose awareness of what was going on that lasted anywhere from seconds to minutes.

It was scary, as on occasions I would find myself in a different place from where I started.

I booked an appointment with my own GP the day after seeing the company doctor. I explained what was happening to my GP and then just broke down. I explained that I had thought I was just tired because of the amount of work I was doing. After a long conversation, he gave me thirteen weeks off work.

Three weeks into the thirteen, I went back to my GP and broke down, sobbing uncontrollably. I told him that I couldn't cope with life anymore.

The doctor thought that I should see a psychologist, as he thought this was an emotional issue rather than a neurological one. He told me he would arrange this. I went home feeling low and unsure of what to do. I became so depressed that I stayed home and didn't want to go out or even answer the phone.

It was a tough time, and I must admit, I didn't think I was going to come out of this one. I recognised the symptoms from when I was in the Merchant Navy. I knew I was starting to go through another breakdown.

I finally received an appointment to see the psychologist. It took a lot of mental effort to go, but even after my first visit I felt a little better. The person I saw was a slim woman with long blonde hair and a soft voice.

I felt at ease from the start and was able to pour out all my feelings and just let go. My emotions got the better of me, and the tears started to flow. At the end of the first session, the psychologist told me that I had said more in the first hour than some patients say in a month. I think this was because she was a stranger and impartial.

Several weeks later, I told her that after about eight weeks off work, the higher management would review my file to see if I was what they called 'long-term sick'. If they thought this was the case, they would send me back to the company doctor with a view to medically retiring me.

After quite a few sessions and some discussion with my psychologist, I managed to convince her that I was fit enough to go back to work. She told me she would agree to me going back to work provided that I telephone her right away if I felt I was slipping back. I said I would.

When I went back to work, my first shift was in the middle of the morning. It was a 9X from Grimsby town centre to Waltham Bradley Road. I took over from the other driver. After taking my fares, I had about two minutes to wait before departing.

I was sitting in the driver's cab looking into the centre mirror at the back of the bus and watching the passengers chatting amongst themselves. I thought, *What a privilege it is that the company trusts me and the other drivers to take passengers from A to B and, in a sense, puts their lives in our hands.*

The strange thing is, it felt different from before I came off work, and this is something I can't explain. I remember when I took the bus over from the other driver, I thanked the Lord I was back doing the job I loved.

I continued seeing the psychologist for about a year. Then she told me that she couldn't take me any further, as she could not find what she called an 'organic reason' why my short-term memory was so poor. She thought it may have been the start of early senile dementia. Being around only fifty four, this was a shock.

After some discussion, she asked me if I would see a psychiatrist. I wasn't sure at the time if this was the way to go, but I said yes.

My first meeting with the consultant psychiatrist was good. He asked me what my symptoms were and how I felt. I told him everything that I had been experiencing.

He told me that I could be suffering from one of two things: mini strokes or latent epilepsy. He advised me not to drive buses until he had performed some tests.

After he told me this, I knew that whatever my diagnosis, my job would be gone. I went to my GP to ask for time off work following the recommendation of the consultant. He gave me another thirteen weeks off.

The full impact would not fully hit me until after a neurologist's final diagnosis.

I underwent an MRI scan and two EEGs. The MRI showed that I had suffered slight brain damage. The first EEG was inconclusive, so a second one was ordered.

I took the second EEG on a Wednesday afternoon. I was tired because this test required me to be awake all night. The electrodes were placed on my head. During a little chat with the operators before the test began, I told them I felt tired. They told me that if I wanted to, I could have a little nap. They woke me some time later. I was groggy and had a headache and felt more tired than I had before my little sleep.

Once I came round properly, I asked them if everything had gone well. They said they couldn't tell me, as they were just the operators. It was up to the doctors to check the findings and report to my consultant.

My doctor was moving about half a mile away, which caused a problem, as it meant I couldn't see the same consultant because he had moved out of my area. Also, my original consultant had gone on holiday and was out of the country.

It would be at least another month before I was able to see a neurologist. During this time, other problems started, and my new consultant psychiatrist diagnosed them as psychosis.

He asked me if I wanted to go on medication for this condition. He advised me that there were many side effects to the medication, which was why doctors asked before prescribing it; however, he said the benefits were worth it.

The doctor read out all the side effects before prescribing the medication and added that the condition could get worse if I didn't go on medication.

Can life get any worse? I thought. I didn't know if I was suffering from mini strokes or epilepsy, and now I had psychosis on top. I must admit, at several points, I wondered whether it was worth continuing in this life.

The medication for psychosis was horrendous. It gave me incredible bouts of tiredness that could come on at any time. I couldn't think straight and felt distant.

If I wanted to go out, someone had to be with me at all times. On one occasion, I was just about to walk across a busy road. The person who was with me grabbed my arm and prevented me from walking straight into an oncoming car.

As a medium, I was used to seeing and hearing Spirit and many other things that were uplifting and pleasant. But with psychosis, I was seeing unpleasant things coming out of the walls and carpets. I heard voices that were threatening and abusive telling me to do unpleasant things.

The medication did help in many ways, I can say for certain. There is a difference between spirit voices and those associated with psychosis. I think because I had worked with Spirit for so long and knew its ways, I could tell the difference.

I was partially sedated for most of the time. Other tablets that I was given did other things. I don't know what they did exactly, but they did help.

Finally, my appointment with a neurologist came though. After waiting so long, I would finally know what I was suffering from and would hopefully be able to move on with my life in some way.

I arrived at Grimsby Diana Princess of Wales Hospital. This was about a fifteen-minute bus ride from where I lived.

The waiting room was quite full, and while I sat there on my own, I wondered how many other people would receive their results today.

About thirty minutes passed, and I watched several people go in and come out of the consultation room.

Then the door opened and a nurse came out and shouted, 'Mr Cork, please!' I stood up and walked towards the door. My heart was racing. The neurologist was a woman of about average build. 'Sit down,' she said assertively. I took a deep breath and sat down across from her desk, which was quite filled with paperwork. The nurse was to my left just out of my vision.

'Now then, tell me what has been happening and your symptoms.'

I went on to explain the loss of awareness, the visual disturbances, and confusion followed by violent headaches after.

'I have all your results here. I have to tell you that you have epilepsy.'

Even though I had prepared to hear this diagnosis or one of mini strokes, it hit me hard. 'Are you sure?' I said.

'Quite sure,' the doctor replied. 'You had a seizure when you were tested the second time, and the MRI confirmed that you have slight brain damage.'

'What happens now?' I asked.

'I will prescribe you medication that should start to slow down the seizures and eventually control them. If you take the medication exactly as I tell you, you should be okay. If you have any problems, go back to your GP. I must also tell you that you cannot drive buses or your car from now on. If the medication controls the seizures and you haven't had one after one year, you can apply to get your car licence.'

I felt like I had been punched hard in the stomach. I felt winded and slightly sick. I wasn't sure if I would be able to stand up, as my legs felt like jelly.

'Is there anything you would like to ask me?' the doctor asked.

I felt terrible anyway, but there were a couple of questions. 'Will I get better?' was my first.

'This can go several ways. One is that the medication may control the condition and you may not have any more seizures. Or it could get worse, in which case we will review your medication,' she said with a slight smile.

'My second question is, when I was a child of about thirteen, I would be, say, writing in class when a mist would gradually build up from the centre of my left eye until I couldn't see out of it. My left arm would start shaking, and I would feel as if I was about to levitate. I would be confused and have difficulty understanding what people said to me. When some of these subsided, I would have this terrific headache and be very tired,' I explained.

'Did you go to your GP?' she asked.

'Yes, I did. He said it was migraines,' I explained.

'No, it wasn't migraines; I don't know how he came to that conclusion. It was definitely epilepsy even then. It sounds like you may have been suffering from it for most of your life.'

I had one more question. 'What kind of epilepsy is it?' I asked.

'Temporal lobe,' she said.

She handed the prescription to me. I stood up and thanked her and left the room. I headed towards the café for a cup of tea and to take in what she had said and to gather my thoughts.

I went to the pharmacy in the hospital to get my medication. Then I caught the bus back into town and walked the short distance to the depot to tell my manager what the diagnosis was.

As a shop steward in our union, I was familiar with the proceedings for employees like myself who were retiring due to a medical condition. It's different when the employee is you, however. The news soon went around the garage, and many of my colleagues were surprised at the results.

I spoke at length with Richard, the assistant operations manager, to find out if there was any other employment that I could do within the company. At the time there wasn't. Ron, the operations manager, did everything to find me something.

I kept calling in to see if there anything. After about a month, a vacancy on what is called the 'backshift' came up. The job entailed sweeping the buses out when they came off the road. The hours were six-thirty in the evening until midnight five days over six. This was good because it meant that I would be off every Sunday.

There was some concern about the medication I was on, as our depot had quite a lot of double-deck buses. What if I had a seizure while at the top of the stairs? Also, if I was working alone and had one, no one would know.

The management and I came to an arrangement. One of our shift fitters had a son who also suffered from epilepsy and knew the signs of a seizure and what to do if I had one.

I was lucky; the medication I was put on started to work quite quickly to control the worst seizures, called grand mals. Put simple, during one of these, I would fall to the floor and shake and so on. My seizures were now mainly confined to petit mals, or drifting.

I was surprised to find that sweeping buses was hard work. You'd think that sweeping up a few tickets would be easy. But it's not just tickets on the floor. I'd find, bottles, cans, paper, plastic bags, old shoes, half-eaten hamburgers, and much more. If a bus needed mopping, that was my job as well.

Some of the old buses had floors like sandpaper. When mopping them, the sweat just poured off me, but it did keep me fit.

It would be nearly one year before I stood on a church rostrum again and was stable enough to apply for my car driving licence.

Fortunately, a medium named Hazel that I had worked with in the past offered me the opportunity to

Jim Cork

work with her until I could drive again. I was pleased, as I was still suffering from petit mals. These didn't last for too long, maybe only seconds, and they didn't cause the adverse effects as they had in the early days.

The other good thing was that if I felt tired after a service, even though Hazel and I shared the work, I could go to sleep on the way home, which I did on many occasions. Sometimes, I gave only two or three messages from the rostrum before feeling tired. Hazel then took the rest of the service.

By the time I started working with Hazel, I was no longer taking the medication for psychosis. My mental state improved to such a degree that I was able to think more clearly. After a period of time, I was able to stop the antipsychotic medication altogether and took just tablets for epilepsy and those for depression.

Before I developed epilepsy, I wasn't prone to moodiness or depression. This condition can cause mental health problems, as it did for me. I still have bad bouts of depression associated with my form of epilepsy. Even at the time of writing, my psychiatrist's opinion is that these bouts will continue for the rest of my life and so will problems with short-term memory.

Life seemed to be getting better as the months rolled by. I enjoyed going to the churches with Hazel, not just because we shared the work but also because we became very close friends and worked as a team.

Unfortunately, nowadays Hazel isn't well enough to travel to the churches, and she cancelled all our bookings for several months.

I took this time to have a break and work out where to go from here. Two or three of the churches telephoned me to ask if I could take services, as Hazel had cancelled.

It has taken time to gain enough confidence to take full services on my own again. I am pleased to say that I am going from strength to strength.

People with epilepsy and similar conditions still face a stigma, which is a shame, as it's not their fault. I encountered one example of this before I developed the condition.

A young fitter where I worked fell to the ground with a grand mal. The manager came running out to witness him shaking and foaming at the mouth on the floor. Several minutes later, the fitter came round, confused and frightened.

Once the young fitter recovered, he carried on with his work. I believe he suffered slight injuries, but they were nothing to worry about and certainly not severe enough to require a trip to hospital.

Around two weeks later, the fitter left the company. Everyone thought he had given his notice in so he could go and work for someone else. The truth is that the manager found a reason to sack him.

Since that time, we have had several changes of depot engineers. When I was offered the job of sweeping the buses, I spoke to this fitter, as he had been re-employed by a successor to his former depot engineer.

While both of us were at work, as he was a shift fitter and also on late turn that night, he asked me why I had moved from driving to the late shift sweeping buses. I told him the story of what had happened and my diagnosis. He told me he, too, suffered from the condition and that I was the only person he had told.

We spoke at length, and he admitted that he felt better for telling someone. He asked me many questions, and I was pleased that I could help in some way. I'm sure it took some pressure off him. I also advised him to tell the management because then we could educate our co-workers on what to do if he had a seizure and they wouldn't be frightened.

Although employers are not supposed to discriminate against people with disabilities, it does go on even today.

I have heard of people who suffer with some form of epilepsy will put that information on their CVs only to receive letters from prospective employers that they have not been successful. You know that as soon as you put down that you suffer from epilepsy on your CV, the hiring firm is going to say no straight away. Having said that, I must say that some employers, like mine, are very good and understanding.

CHAPTER 21

BACK ON THE ROAD

J ust recently, Sandra and I travelled to a church to attend the Open Circle. I worked this church on many occasions before I developed epilepsy.

The people were very welcoming, and those giving messages were excellent. They gave first-class evidential mediumship.

In this church, a medium giving a message stands up and walks over to the recipient of the message. In other churches, mediums sit while giving messages.

We arrived in good time, as I like to. The church was still closed when we arrived. At my own church, when people are on duty, they arrive to open the doors at least three-quarters of an hour before a service because some people come from a long way away, and like me, they like to set off in good time. Also, we don't like people waiting outside any longer than they have to.

I think Sandra and I only had to wait about ten minutes. A group of about six had joined us. Shortly after, a car pulled up, and one of those who were on duty opened the doors.

The church was just as I had remembered it, although for some strange reason, it looked smaller. I think this was because the chairs were arranged in a square rather than in a circle. In my own church the chairs are always arranged in a circle. I think I like them better in a square.

Looking round, I saw only two people that I recognised. I thought it was going to be a good night, and I had been looking forward to this all week.

At seven, one of the ladies in the front row said, 'Good evening, everyone, and welcome to our Open Circle. Is there anyone that has not been to an Open Circle before?'

The room was silent.

'Good. Just to set a few ground rules first. The Open Circle is for everyone to work that wishes to do so. We have fledglings in the circle who are practising. If they come to you, just answer with a yes, I don't know, or I don't understand. Please don't give them your life story, as it is up to them to give the information to you.'

After a slight pause, she continued, 'May we sing hymn number seven, standing, all those who can?' After the hymn, the chairperson then opened in prayer and then asked for absent healing. 'Thank you, and now I declare your circle open.'

There was a pause of fifteen seconds or so. 'Don't all speak at once,' she said with a slight giggle. It's always nice to have a little humour to break the silence.

A man in the front row and to my left stood up, took a few paces forwards, and turned to face a woman.

'Can I come to you, please?' he said with a smile on his face. I think he was in his mid-sixties. I guess he was around five feet six inches tall, and he was portly. He spoke softly but was loud enough to be heard at the back of the room.

His descriptions of people in the spirit world were very detailed. The young lady he talked to was very excited by what he said. It had been a long time since I had heard a medium give such detail.

I gained a lot of work in churches through their Open Circles, as this allowed them to see me work before booking me. I am pleased to say that I am gaining back most of the churches that I lost.

Sandra goes with me to quite a few of my bookings now, and I'm sure she enjoys it. I had asked her in the past if she wanted to come to one or two, but until recently, she always said that she would think about it.

I'm glad she comes along now. Her psychic abilities have come out more. If I remember correctly, they first started when Madeline died.

She told me when I visited that she heard footsteps going from her daughter Tracy's bedroom to her son Lee's who were not home at the time. At first I thought she may have imagined it.

One afternoon on one of my visits, I was having a cup of tea with her when I heard footsteps going from one room to another. I said, 'Oh, is Tracy in, or is that Lee?'

'It's just the two of us,' she said with a slight smile.

I got up walked towards the stairs. As I approached Tracy's room, a cold shiver went up and down my spine. I looked in all the rooms and saw nothing. I went downstairs.

'Told you. Now do you believe me?' Sandra said, a little smile just showing through.

'I really did hear footsteps,' I insisted.

'It's just Mom having a walkabout,' Sandra said almost laughing.

This was the second time I heard footsteps, and so clearly. They sounded like the real thing. Like everything in this field, you need to experience this for yourself.

Sandra has slowly improved her sensitivity. It would be nice if her ability came out in her as mine did. The one thing you need is confidence, and that only comes with time.

CHAPTER 22

A GREAT LOSS

On Wednesday, 24 September 1997, I decided to go to the Open Circle at my own church. I finished work early, so I had plenty of time to unwind. I brought along several music books and played the piano for a while.

Several of our members knew I went early and would often come down for a sing-along. For some reason, I was making quite a few mistakes. I apologised to them and passed it off as being a little tired.

At the end of the Open Circle, I had a cup of tea and then went round to see Tony S. to make sure everything was all right, as he had had a cold. He suffered from chronic lung disease, so complications could set in.

I put my key in the door at Tony's house, but it wouldn't turn. I took it out and tried again but it still wouldn't work. I thought he may have left his key in the lock, so I lifted up the letter box and shouted, 'Come on, you lazy bugger! You've left the key in the door.'

I heard him grunt. I thought he may have just woken up, as he often used to catnap on the sofa. I waited for a while but heard nothing more. I thought maybe he had fallen asleep again.

I walked round to the front to peer through the window, as he lived in a small sheltered-accommodation flat. I couldn't see him through the thick net curtains. If he planned to go out, he would have told me when I saw him the night before.

I walked back to the other door and tried my key again. This time the key turned the lock. A cold shiver went down my spine, as I knew for certain that the key hadn't turned the lock on the previous two tries.

I opened the door, and straight away I couldn't feel any life force. It was so silent. I walked down the short hallway to the living room, passing the kitchen on the way.

I pushed the living room door open and turned to my right. The sofa on the back wall was obscured by the door when I first walked in. I turned to the right and caught a glimpse of his back, which was turned towards me. Tony S. was sitting on the sofa, his legs crossed and his arms by his sides. His head was leaning to the left.

As I turned further to the right to see him in full view, it was obvious that he had died.

I sat for about half an hour talking to him and trying to sort out who to telephone first. It was 9.20 p.m. when

I found him and around 9.50 when I made the first call to the doctor. The answerphone gave me the number for emergencies, as it was after hours.

Next I called his sister, who lived in Birmingham. Third, I called Lillian, who broke down over the phone in disbelief.

After a period, the doorbell rang. It was the Doctor. I recognised him when I saw him. He too had visited the ELMS on occasion. He informed me as this was a sudden death, he would have to inform the police. He said just before he left that he thought Tony had suffered a massive heart attack. He wouldn't have felt a thing; death would have been instantaneous. The doctor added that a post-mortem would be needed to determine the exact cause of death, however.

Within about an hour, things were well under way. The undertakers had been informed, and they, too, were on their way. Once they arrived, they took all the details and then took Tony S. away in a private ambulance. It wasn't long before I was left on my own.

I just sat there reflecting on the journey that Tony S. and I had taken over twenty-seven years. How far we both had come in that time. My spiritual mentor had gone home.

He was brilliant at philosophy and believed completely in life after death and in reincarnation. Not being a medium himself, he had always admired those with the gift.

It was around 11.40 p.m. when I left the flat to go home to Lillian. The next day I called at the flat to take some things out. The lady that lived above caught my attention and asked if she could have a word.

'Of course,' I said.

She explained that in the very early hours of Thursday morning, she heard Tony S. singing his head off. He sang 'The Battle Hymn of the Republic', the ELMS anthem that we sang before each meeting. I explained that it was imposable, as Tony S. had died and had been taken by the undertakers around 11 p.m. on the Wednesday night.

The woman's face drained. She was adamant that she had heard Tony S. singing and added that she thought he had such a good voice, although he sang a bit loudly for that time of morning.

If ever I needed proof, there it was. The woman upstairs, as far as I know, was not religious. She and Tony hardly spoke in the few years that Tony lived in the flat. The woman certainly would not have known that 'The Battle Hymn of the Republic' was Tony's favourite song.

At the funeral, the crematorium was packed, standing room only. Tony S. was loved by many people, and it showed on that day. I was privileged to take part in the service.

You don't realise how important a person is in your life until he or she is gone. Tony's passing left a big hole in many people's hearts, one that would never be filled.

Several speaker's secretaries were there. They told me that when they telephoned him to confirm my booking, they spent many hours talking to him and would miss that.

Tony S. never believed he was a medium or mediumistic; however, if upon meeting a person for the first time his tummy played up, giving him a strange sensation inside, he knew instinctively if that person was good or not. I can't remember a time when it let him down.

He may not have been a medium in the strict sense of the word, but his sixth sense was second to none. Nobody I've met over the last thirty-five years has come close to his accuracy.

Since he passed on, there has not been anyone who I can talk to in such depth or for as long as I could talk with him. He was a true teacher, philosopher, and great man of our time.

Tony's memory will live on in many ways. One way is in the friends he made over the years that are still with us. Another is through the cine club members that I see from time to time who still talk about him, and, of course, through the films he made.

About two years before Tony S. died, he asked me if we could go down to Southend-on-Sea to see some relatives he had not seen for a very long time. I said we could and arranged it. We had a very good holiday, and Tony really was pleased that he had seen them.

We had to be careful what we said because they were Catholic, and we didn't want to upset them with our beliefs. Nothing could have been further from the truth.

After we came back, Tony received a phone call from them to say how nice it was to see him again.

I enjoyed the holiday as well and joined in a lot of the conversations, even though the topics were mainly confined to Tony and his family.

Tony told me that part of the telephone conversation after we returned had been about beliefs, as some of his relatives were elderly. It came out that Tony and I were Spiritualists.

They told Tony they would have loved a reading, and one of them knew I was a medium. They asked, if we were to go down again, if I would give them a reading. Of course, Tony said yes.

It also emerged that some relatives who had moved to Canada had similar beliefs to ours. After some time, it was suggested that Tony and I go over and stay with them, as they had plenty of room, so we could save on hotel bills as we had a holiday of a lifetime.

The main problem was arranging a flight for Tony, who had emphysema. After contacting many airlines, he found only one that was prepared to take him at that time. It may be different now.

After a lot of planning, Tony and I arranged to spend around ten days in Canada. I would serve a few Spiritualist churches while we were there, and Tony would contact the speaker's secretaries to arrange this.

It wasn't to be. Tony died about a year before we were due to fly out. I know from the way he had talked about the trip that it would have been the absolute highlight of his life.

Many people were saddened that we couldn't make it. It didn't seem right for me to go without Tony, and I'm pleased I wasn't asked. Not because I didn't want to go—it would have been the highlight of my life too—but because a big part of me wouldn't have been there. After all, Tony and I had been working together for around twenty years.

CHAPTER 23

THE FUTURE

Many people have asked me where I want to go from here. This is always a difficult question to answer. I tell them I still have a great deal to learn. We never stop learning.

I love this work; I always have and always will. It would be a privilege to work in more halls and theatres. Many years ago, I gave readings on a radio station and was a guest on another station answering questions on the paranormal and remote viewing.

This was a challenge, as I was not quite prepared for the in-depth questions thrown at me. However, both appearances went very well, and I was asked if I would speak on another two other occasions. I said yes and loved it.

I will carry on progressing in this life, sharing and giving the best evidence I can on the continuation of life after this physical one, until I go home to be reunited with my loved ones in the spirit world.

When I'm giving a private reading and the subject asks me what the future will be, I ask, 'Has anything changed in the last two years?' If the answer is no, I say that nothing will change in the next two unless the person helps to create change.

At the end of the day, all of us have choices. I will go on for as long as I can serving Spirit as well as mankind.

There is so much that we don't understand at this point in time. I'm sure as science progresses, some of the mysteries will be unravelled, but until then, I, like you, will be searching for the answers.

There's beauty in everything if we care to look. I hope the choices you make will bring what you need to your life, as they have in mine. God bless.

The End

About the Author

Jim Cork has been working as a Spiritualist medium for over thirty-five years alongside full-time jobs. Now for the first time he has opened his heart in his autobiography. He nearly died at only thirteen months old but pulled through thanks to his adoptive parents. For many years, he led a quiet life until Spirit called him to service. Jim studied his craft in a closed development group for many years and has taught many students to be mediums. When he was fifty-four, illness turned his life upside down. This in turn led to a breakdown. Not to be beaten, Jim fought to have as normal a life as possible. Jim is a truly inspiring person who takes nothing for granted. Modest in every sense of the word, he beautifully articulates Spirit's message to his recipients, bringing words of comfort, hope, and uplift to those in need.

Respected by his peers and co-workers, Jim admits he is still learning. Although still struggling with health issues, he strives to be a better ambassador for Spirit and those whom he comes into contact with.

About the Book

Communicating with the World Unseen, Jim Cork's autobiography, highlights his life from birth to the present day. As he talks about the two families in his life, he reflects on events that caused joy and pain. Jim takes readers through a period in which peace could only be gained by leaving home. The development of his mediumship on his return had already been mapped out by Spirit. The group that Jim joined trained him in all sorts of spiritual phenomena, including some he could only dream of. As Jim was developing, he went through one of his most difficult times as he suffered from epilepsy. Jim explains the impact his diagnosis had on his work life and on his personal life. The death of one of the most important people in Jim's life, Tony S., Jim's spiritual mentor and manager for twenty-seven years, turned Jim's world upside down again. Jim's life has been filled with ups and downs. Spirit has never been far behind him, as you will learn, and will be there for all of us.

Lightning Source UK Ltd.
Milton Keynes UK
UKOW051632180113

205098UK00001B/2/P